MUSIC
and
KABBALAH

MUSIC
and
KABBALAH

MATITYAHU GLAZERSON

A JASON ARONSON BOOK

ROWMAN & LITTLEFIELD PUBLISHERS, INC.
Lanham • Boulder • New York • Toronto • Plymouth, UK

A JASON ARONSON BOOK

ROWMAN & LITTLEFIELD PUBLISHERS, INC.

Published in the United States of America
by Rowman & Littlefield Publishers, Inc.
A wholly owned subsidary of The Rowman & Littlefield Publishing Group, Inc.
4501 Forbes Boulevard, Suite 200, Lanham, Maryland 20706
www.rowmanlittlefield.com

Estover Road
Plymouth PL6 7PY
United Kingdom

Copyright © 1997 by Matityahu Glazerson.
First Rowman & Littlefield edition 2006

British Library Cataloguing in Publication Information Available

Library of Congress Cataloging-in-Publication Data

Glazerson, Matityahu.
  [Musikah ve-kabalah.   English]
  Music and Kabbalah / by Matityahu Glazerson.
    p.   cm.
  Originally published: Music and Kabbala. Jerusalem : M. Glazerson. 1988.
  ISBN 1-56821-933-4 (alk. paper)
  1. Music and Cabala.   I. Title.
  ML3195.G5313   1996
  780.0296—dc21   96-49286

Manufactured in the United States of America. Jason Aronson Inc. offers books and
cassettes. For information and catalog write to Jason Aronson Inc., 230 Livingston
Street, Northvale, New Jersey 07647.

Contents

PART THREE
THE MUSICAL INSTRUMENTS

Preface

Music and Kabbalah was written as a result of a series of lectures given on this topic. The lectures aroused such a great interest that it was decided to compile and arrange these lectures into book form.

The purpose of this book is to enlighten and reveal the depth of the wisdom of Judaism and the holy language that embraces all spheres of life, music included. My other books discuss various subjects highlighting the wisdom of the Hebrew language, through the analysis of words and letters, as is reflected in different cultures (*From Hinduism Back to Judaism*); astrology (*Above the Zodiac*); economy (*Riches and Righteousness*); and the relationship between husband and wife (*Revelations About Marriage*).

Music is important to attaining a prophetic state. This idea can be found in numerous instances in the Bible itself, as, for instance, in the case of Elisha the prophet (2 Kings, 3:15): ועתה קחו לי מנגן והי–ה כנגן המנגן ותה–י עליו יד ה'; "Now bring me a musician. And it was that when the musician played, the hand of Hashem came upon him." About this expression, כנגן המנגן, Rabbi Nachman of Breslav says that a musician should reach a level whereby he and the melody become one.

Another example is found in connection with the prophet Samuel and King Saul when Samuel told Saul (1 Samuel, 10:5): כבאך שם העיר ופגעת חבל נביאים ירדים מהבמה ולפני–הם נבל ותף וחליל וכנור מתנבאים; "And when you will come to the city you shall meet a band of prophets coming from a high place with a harp, drum, flute, and lyre, and they will be prophesying themselves." Through music, the prophet draws prophetic energy from the upper worlds. About אסף

(Asaph), הימן (Heiman), and ידותון (Yedutun), it is written (1 Chronicles, 25:1) that they used to prophesy with musical instruments, as is said: לבני אסף והימן וידותון המתנבאים בכנרות בנבלים ובמצלתם; "And the sons of Asaph, and Heiman, and Yedutun used to prophesy with harps, lutes, and their cymbals."

This book is not meant to cover all the related aspects of this subject; these are very vast and deep, being connected with many complicated terms in Kabbalah. Our aim is to instill in the hearts of the people the idea that the divine, holy language with which God created the world contains abundant knowledge. Those who have a desire to know more will have to seek it in different places. My purpose is merely to open people's minds and hearts to the spring of treasures in Judaism. Unfortunately, many people do not realize this today and, hence, look for the divine truth in the East and elsewhere, not realizing that the source lies so close to them—in Judaism itself.

My hope is that this book, with God's help, will contribute to a deeper understanding and awareness of the truth of the living Torah, bringing appreciation and, hence, fulfillment. This knowledge will consequently return God's "children" back to their "Father in heaven," ultimately hastening the redemption, bringing the Messiah speedily in our days.

Rabbi Matityahu Glazerson
Jerusalem
Tammuz 5748

Introduction

When presented with an unfamiliar piece of music, a musician will search a page of notes for a sign to inform him as to which tempo is appropriate for that movement. Fast, slow, upbeat, melancholy, grave, moderate; he will use the term to set the pace of the song. Now, suppose you were a musician and the term that confronted you was "religious," "pious," or "spiritual." At what pace would you set the tune? To me, these terms are synonymous with "lively," "joyous," or "cheerful." Indeed, when a person reflects upon the wondrous beauties of the world in which God has placed us, and the constant gifts that shower down from heaven upon our unworthy heads, he cannot help but burst into joyous songs of praise to the holy Creator. The Torah itself admonishes us for not having served with gladness (Deuteronomy, 28:47): "When you had plenty of everything you would not serve Hashem your God with happiness and a glad heart." From this verse we see that one must serve God with joy and gladness, and that this may include song (*Erchin*, 11a).

There are countless examples of spiritual giants who have used song as an intrinsic part of their divine worship.

The Midrash Rabbah (Vayetzei) says that during the twenty-two years that our Patriarch Jacob tended Laban's flocks, he praised God with resplendent songs. The wind carried these arias with them for almost a thousand years before they were finally revealed to King David. At midnight David would awaken to the sounds of a northern wind playing his harp, which was suspended above his head, as it says (Psalms, 119:62): "I will rise at midnight to praise you . . . ." Thus, our holy king was inspired to compose beautiful psalms to the King of Kings, and these songs have inspired others for thousands of years.

Music has always had the ability to uplift and to influence. When asked how he was able to change the lives of so many lost Jews, the eminent luminary Rabbi Meir Shapiro of Lublin (1887–1934) replied: "If one goes to a wedding, he may arrive in a bad mood, but the musical band will instantly lift his spirits. I carry around the band inside me all the time!"

King David said (Psalms, 100:2): "Serve God with joy, come before him with song." Let us examine what song is and what it can do so that we can fully employ this powerful and delightful tool in our divine service.

Rabbi Refael Harris

PART ONE

The Musical Scale

CHAPTER 1

The Seven-letter Cycle

The musical scale is made up of seven notes: do; re; mi; fa; sol; la; ti. These notes are then repeated on a higher scale; then again on a higher scale, ad infinitum. Each seven-note scale is equal to one cycle. In Judaism, the number seven is significant for several reasons. One is that there are seven kabbalistic spheres (ספירות, *sefirot*) each of which corresponds to one week of the Omer, which itself is seven weeks of seven days each, from Passover to Shavuot. Each letter of the Hebrew alphabet is parallel to a different note of the scale, and hence to the appropriate sphere. Each sphere has its own position to the right, left, or middle. Therefore, the corresponding letters of the alphabet, and the notes of the scale, are in the same position as their complementary sphere.

The letter א and the note "do," both being first, are parallel to the sphere חסד (*chesed,* lovingkindness), and are positioned accordingly on the right. The ב and the re are parallel to גבורה (*gevurah,* strength), on the left; the ג and the mi to תפארת (*tiferet,* beauty), which is placed in the middle, and as such represents balance and harmony. Further, the letter ד and the note fa correspond to נצח (*netzach,* eternity) on the right; ה and sol, equal to הוד (*hod,* glory), on the left; ו and la, יסוד (*yesod,* foundation), in the middle; ז and ti, מלכות (*malchut,* kingdom), also in the middle. The notes then continue on a higher octave, and the alphabet continues accordingly: ח equal to do; ט to re; and so on. Hence, each letter of the alphabet relates to a different sphere and is in a specific position.

Left	Middle	Right
גבורה		חסד
re		do
	תפארת	
	mi	
הוד		נצח
sol		fa
	יסוד	
	la	
	מלכות	
	ti	

It is interesting to note that the difference between the major key and the minor key is explained by the building up of the notes in the key. In the minor key, the middle tones (i.e., the mi and the la) are nearer to the left side (being only a semitone away), which is the side representing the heart.

Major			Minor		
גבורה		חסד	גבורה		חסד
re		do	re		do
	תפאדת			תפאדת	
	mi			mi	
הוד		נצח	הוד		נצח
sol		fa	sol		fa
	יסוד			יסוד	
	la			la	
	מלכות			מלכות	
	ti			ti	

The Hebrew words for the three positions of the spheres are אמצע (emtza, middle); ימין (yemin, right); and שמאל (smol, left). The initials of these words spell the word איש (ish, man). איש (ish) has the connotation of the perfect man; for example, Moses is called איש הא–להים (ish HaElokim "man of God": Deuteronomy, 33:1; also Psalms, 90:1; Samuel, 2:27; 9:6; 1 Kings, 12:22; 31:1; 2 Kings, 1:13, 4:9; Nehemiah, 12:24; 2 Chronicles, 25:7). Consequently, we see that when the middle, right, and left are together, they form a perfect combination.

The spheres also represent מידות (*midot,* divine attributes), through which we understand God's actions and creations. In astrology, the seven מידות (*midot*) that we have seen are parallel to the seven מזלות (*mazalot,* celestial bodies: see chart, p. xx). Jupiter is parallel to חסד (*chesed*), the first sphere, on the right, and to the letter א; Mars corresponds to גבורה (*gevurah*), the second sphere on the left, and to ב; the sun to תפארת (*tipheret*) in the middle and to ג; Venus to נצח (*netzach*) and to ד; Mercury to הוד (*hod*) and to ה; the moon to יסוד (*yesod*) and to ו; and Earth to מלכות (*malchut*) and to ז. (The planet–music relationship will be explained later.)

According to the Ramchal (Rabbi Moshe Chaim Luzzatto) in his book *Adir BaMarom* (p. 40), the planets are moved by musical waves. These are his words: "All those things above are carried out by music, and all the luminaries, when they go out from their source, are motivated by music." Each planet has its music. It is interesting to note that scientists have recently discovered that each planet produces a different melody. As has been seen, according to the Ramchal, it is really the music itself that affects and, hence, moves the planets.

The *Zohar* (Exodus, Shlach) says that the constellations themselves create music. And, according to the *Zohar* (Exodus, Vayakel), the music of the sun is so wonderful that if the ears of man were not blocked, he would be capable of hearing this music. He would not, however, be able to exist, for his soul would leave his body. The Rambam, in his book *The Guide for the Perplexed* (part 2, ch. 8) also mentions this and other theories of how the stars create different sounds.

Interestingly, the major key is the plan of the cycle of the nineteen years that contain seven leap years. The seven leap years occur on the third, the sixth, the eighth, the eleventh, the fourteenth, the seventeenth, and the nineteenth years, respectively. Observing the order of these years, one may notice that they follow the same sequence as the intervals between the notes (or tones) in the major key; for example, two years correspond to one tone—between the do and the re there is a "full space," a tone. When there is only a one-year difference, this relates to the semitone—for example, the space between the mi and the fa.

The seven-note–letter cycle is also parallel to the seven shepherds of Israel: Abraham, Isaac, Jacob, Moses, Aaron, Joseph, and David. This is the order in which they are led as guests into the sukkah on the seven days of the festival of Sukkot. Hence Abraham, whose attribute was חסד (*chesed*), is the first, corresponding to the do and the sphere of חסד (*chesed,* lovingkindness). Joseph, whose attribute was צדקות (*tzidkut,* righteousness) is the sixth, parallel to the la and the sphere of יסוד (*yesod*). ו, the sixth letter, also represents the צדיק (*tzaddik,* righteous man) since it stands for a straight line between heaven and earth. This helps us understand the verse in Proverbs (10:25): צדיק יסוד עולם; "The righteous one is the foundation of the world." Indeed, when a violinist tunes his instrument, he tunes it to the sixth note, la, which, as we have seen, represents "foundation."

The last note of the scale, the ti, corresponds to the seventh letter of the alphabet, ז, and to Shabbat, the seventh day of the week. These are parallel to the attribute of מלכות (*malchut,* kingdom), as Shabbat attests to God's kingdom on earth. The Jewish people, by keeping the Sabbath properly, testify to God's having created the world in seven days. This is one reason why one who keeps the Sabbath is regarded as though he kept all the *mitzvot* (Shemot Rabbah, end Parsha, 25; Talmud Yerushalmi, *Brachot,* 9a, ch. 1, law 5).

The alphabet continues above ז as the notes continue on a higher scale. The scale is repeated for a third time to complete the alphabet; the first seven notes consist of the letters from א to ז, the second from ח to נ, and the last scale from ס to ש. The letter ת is not represented, as it is one above the number seven, representing the number eight.

Note	3	2	1	Planet	Attribute	Place	Shepherd
do	ס	ח	א	Jupiter	חסד	right	Abraham
re	ע	ט	ב	Mars	גבורה	left	Isaac
mi	פ	י	ג	sun	תפארת	middle	Jacob
fa	צ	כ	ד	Venus	נצח	right	Moses
sol	ק	ל	ה	Mercury	הוד	left	Aaron
la	ר	מ	ו	moon	יסוד	middle	Joseph
ti	ש	נ	ז	Earth	מלכות	middle	David

In the second scale, the same principles apply. The ח, which stands for חיים (*chayim,* life), signifies the note do in a higher key, and the attribute חסד (*chesed*), and hence is on the right. The ט stands for טהרה (*taharah,* purity), which is analogous to re and גבורה (*gevurah*), and is on the left. The י matches mi and תפארת (*tiferet*), and is in the middle, etc.

We see, then, that the second scale is of a similar structure to the first.

The last seven letters forming the third scale are constructed in the same manner: ס, do, חסד (*chesed,* lovingkindness), on the right; ע, re, גבורה (*gevurah,* strength), on the left; פ, mi, תפארת (*tiferet,* beauty), in the middle; צ, fa, נצח (*netzach,* eternity), on the right; ק, sol, הוד (*hod,* glory), on the left; ר, la, יסוד (*yesod,* foundation), in the middle; and ש, ti, מלכות (*malchut,* kingdom), in the middle. The book *Hafla'a* by the Baal HaKane says that the exact same insight and erudition that applies to connecting letters into words, also applies to connecting notes into song.

The *Tikunei Zohar* mentions three things that music affects: the Torah, the *Shechina* (the divine glory), and the *Geula* (redemption). These three things, in turn, are parallel to the mind, heart, and body, respectively. First, the Torah represents the מח (*moach,* the mind, brain). This is because music has the power to open one's mind and improve one's שכל (*seichel,* mind). In his book *Pirkei Hatzlacha,* the Rambam (Rabbi Moshe ben Maimon, fifteenth century) writes that if a man wants to feel elevated, he should sing. Singing has the power to elevate a man as it opens his mind. The Gemara says that one should learn Torah with music (a tune), as this aids one's studies. Hence, one can frequently hear men learning in a sing-song manner in *yeshivah.*

Second, the *Shechina* represents the לב (*lev,* heart). Similarly, the בית המקדש (*Beit HaMikdash,* the Temple), represents the heart. The ancient Levites and prophets used music so that the *Shechina* would descend upon them.

Third, the *Geula* represents the כבד (*kaved,* liver), which itself represents the גוף (*guf,* body). The Jewish people were redeemed with music when God took them out of Egypt, as we see in Exodus (14:32): אז ישיר משה ובני ישראל את השירה הזאת לה; "Then Moses and the children of Israel chose to sing this song to God." The Torah does not use the verb שר (*shar,* sang), but rather ישיר (*yashir,* will sing). Rashi (Rabbi Shlomo ben Yitzchak, the famous eleventh-century talmudic scholar) says this means that in messianic times the righteous Jews who died will be brought back to life and will sing again.

This idea is further illustrated in the sequence of the three scales. The first scale, from א to ז, represents the כבד (*kaved,* liver); the middle scale, from ח to נ, represents the לב (*lev,* heart); the third scale, ס to ש, the מח (*moach,* brain). The first scale elevates the physical body and world into the second-higher scale, which in turn leads to the third. The order of the daily prayers prescribed in the Jewish סדור (*siddur,* prayer book) progresses in a like manner. The morning blessings lead into the Pesukei d'Zimra, songs and psalms of praise, which lead into the recitation of the Shema, the declaration of God's unity. These lead up to, and prepare one's emotions for, the final Shemona Esrei (the eighteen benedictions), which represents the intellect and the perfection of man.

The initials of כבד (*kaved*), לב (*lev*), and מח (*moach*) form the word מלך (*melech,* king) and the word כלם (*kulam,* all). This indicates that perfection is obtained by unifying these three aspects. The numerical value (*gematria*) of מלך is 90 (מ = 40; ל = 30; כ = 20). Ninety is also the value of the letter צ, which represents צדיק (*tzaddik,* righteous man), who symbolizes purity. The lower numerical value (found by adding the digits together to obtain one figure) is 9 (90 = 9 + 0 = 9). Nine, being the highest numeral, represents the highest level. We can deduce, then, that through the unification of these three components one may realize perfection and fulfillment.

CHAPTER 2

The Hebrew Vowels

According to Kabbalah, the Hebrew vowels have profound significance. Abulafia, a great Jewish mystic, said that the shape of each vowel portrays its specific quality and nature. The vowels are made up of lines and dots, and each one represents a different sphere.

Vowel	Name	Sound		Sphere
ָ	קמץ	aw	כתר	crown
	פתח	ah	חכמה	wisdom
ֵ	צרה	ai	בינה	understanding
ֶ	סגול	eh	חסד	lovingkindness
ְ	שוא	end or beginning	גבורה	strength
וֹ	חולם	oh	תפארת	beauty
	חיריק	ee	נצח	eternity
	קובוץ	ew	הוד	glory
וּ	שורוק	oo	יסוד	foundation
	אות	—	מלכות	kingdom

The קמץ (*kamatz*), which is a combination of both the line and the dot, is on the highest level, as it corresponds to the highest sphere, כתר (*keter,* crown). Hebrew words have a three-letter root from which their meaning is derived. The word קמץ is the root of the word קמוץ (*kamutz,* closed). This indicates that the vowel's corresponding sphere, כתר, is hidden and distant; it is closed off from us.

In contrast, the open line, the פתח (*patach*), represents פתוח (*patuach*, open), as the mouth is open when pronouncing this vowel. It is on par with the sphere of חכמה (*chochma*, wisdom), and we can see this connection in the verse: פותח את ידך; "Open Your hand" (Psalms, 145:16). The word ידך (*yadcha*, Your hand) refers to the letter יוד (Yud; י). The letters of the word יוד are similar to those of the word יד (*yad*, hand), and its shape is similar to that of a hand. The sphere that is represents is חכמה, which is positioned on the right side on the map of spheres; hence, this vowel represents the opening to the letters of the alphabet.

The vowel consisting of two dots, the צירה (*tzairai*), is like a concentration of the line and is on the left side. In Kabbalah, something very concentrated is called גבורה (*gevurah*, strength) and בינה (*bina*, understanding). Like a pair of eyes, this vowel represents deep understanding.

The vowel סגול (*segol*), which represents חסד (*chesed*, loving-kindness), is on the right side. To pronounce this sound, the mouth is open. This is directly related to חסד, which is akin to openheartedness. The word חֶסֶד is written with two סגולs under the ח and the ס.

The שוא (*shva*), which is positioned on the left, normally stops or starts a syllable. This ability is characteristic of גבורה (*gevurah*, strength).

חולם (*cholam*) has the same root in its name as the word החלמה (*hachlama*, recuperation). This vowel is parallel to the sphere תפאדת (*tiferet*, beauty or harmony), positioned in the middle, which itself refers to health. The dot on top indicates divine influence from above.

The חיריק (*chirik*) is a single dot that represents remoteness, or something distant. It is also parallel to the sphere of נצח (*netzach*, eternity), which is a concept remote and distant from man.

The קובוץ (*kubutz*), three dots, has the same root as the word קבץ (*kibutz*, gathering), as the sphere הוד (*hod*, glory) to which it corresponds is a gathering of light.

The שורוק (*shuruk*) has its root in the word שרק, which has the same letter and, hence, is connected to the word קשר (*kesher*, joining). This refers to Joseph, who joined and united the twelve tribes of Israel (Genesis, 45:21).

The tenth sphere of מלכות (*malchut*, kingdom) does not represent a specific vowel, but is a combination of them all.

Thus, we see the significance of the shape and sound of the vowels, and how they relate to their nature.

In the alphabet, the א and ב are the opening letters; they are parallel on the musical scale to the notes do and re, which open every scale. א and ב also form the word אב (*av,* father), as the father is the influencing force, and the root of everything.

The letter "a," the first letter in the English alphabet, is derived from the Hebrew א. The mouth is open when pronouncing this sound. The letter א, as well as the note do, is the opening for everything, and appropriately represents חסד (*chesed,* lovingkindness). Lovingkindness is manifested by open hands, open heart, and open doors, and is the proper way to open a relationship between people.

חסד (*chesed*) is positioned on the right side. As we will see, those attributes positioned on the right, left, or middle relate to others of the same position.

The vowel appertaining to the letter ב is the צרה (*tzairai*). The ב and the note re represent גבורה (*gevurah,* strength), positioned on the left side. The ג represents תפארת (*tiferet,* beauty) and, together with mi, is in the middle.

The letter ד (דֶלֶת, Dalet, which also spells דֶלֶת, *delet,* door), which is also pronounced with a פתח (*patach,* which also spells פֶתַח, *petach,* an opening), once again represents an opening together with the fa, both being on the right side (see p. xx). The letter ה (as well as sol) is similar to ב, as it, too, has a צרה (*tzairai*) as its vowel sound, and relates to גבורה (*gevurah,* strength), הוד (*hod,* glory), and בינה (*bina,* understanding), all on the left. The ו and the la, and the ז and ti, have a קמץ (*kamatz*) and a פתח (*patach*), respectively, and are both in the middle.

In the musical scale, the do (א) and the fa (ד) are on the right side. As we have seen, the א and ד both have a פתח (*patach*); hence, the do and fa represent opening. On the left side are the ב (re) and the ה (sol), both having a צירה (*tzairai*) as their vowel sounds, and both representing contraction or constriction.

As the letter ב stops the א from expansion, so the note re stops the do. The ג and the mi indicate harmony, as it is the balance between the two. Similarly, the sol stops the fa from expansion.

The la corresponds to the letter ו, which is parallel to יסוד (*yesod,* foundation). The ו has a קמץ (*kamatz*), a combination of a line and dot, which represents the crown, as the sphere of כתר (*keter,* crown) is the highest of the spheres in the middle and יסוד is the lowest of the spheres in the middle. The ti, the seventh note—equal to ז, the seventh letter—is the culmination of everything, as after ti a new scale starts. The same idea is seen in שבת (Shabbat, the Sabbath), the seventh day, which is the apex of the previous week and a preparation for the new one.

CHAPTER 3

Relationship Between the Higher and Lower Octaves

The Talmud (*Shabbat*, 104a) states that the letters א, ח, and ס are interchangeable, being the first notes (the dos) of each scale (see chart, p. xx). The ב, ט, and ע are interchangeable, as they are the res; and so on.

All the letters of the Hebrew alphabet are parallel to the spheres. The א, ח, and ס—the first, eighth, and fifteenth letters—are all parallel to the same sphere, חסד (*chesed,* lovingkindness). Consequently, they are interchangeable, as the same concept underlies them all. For example, the letter א stands for אולפן (*ulpan,* learning), acquiring wisdom. ח stands for חיים (*chayim,* life). ס betokens סומך (*somech,* support), as we see in Psalms (145:14): סומך הי לכל הנופלים; "God supports the fallen," indicating His aspect of being a basis for all. Hence, the א, ח, and ס all represent ideas of being a base—that is, learning, life, and support are all a basis for higher living. These three letters are parallel to the sphere of חסד.

The word חסד (*chesed,* lovingkindness) is made up of two terms: חס-ד; חס (*chas,* having mercy), on the דל (*dal,* the poor). All these letters are positioned on the right side and, therefore, denote expansion.

The letters ב, ט, and ע are also interchangeable, one to the other, as they all correspond to the note re of their respective scales. These letters are on the left side, which represents contraction. Note the similarity between the Hebrew word "left" (שמאל, *smol*) and the English word "small." These three letters also spell the word טבע

13

(*teva*, nature). Let us examine why these three letters, specifically, spell the word for nature.

The ב represents a house, a container, an enclosing body, a shell that protects and encloses the internal. The word ב (*Bet*), בית (*beiit*), itself is a house. Even the shape hints at its meaning, as it has a top, bottom, opening, and wall. We have seen that the א "opens," and the ב "closes" (see "The Hebrew Vowels," p. 27). The word בריא (*bari*, healthy), is made up of two terms, ב-ריא; the ב (the body) contains ריא, air; ריא is on par with אויר (*avir*, air). (Notice that the English word "air" comes from the Hebrew אויר). This is a principle that has found its way into yoga: that breathing is a most essential aspect of health. So, a healthy person is one who contains the element of air in his body and is breathing properly.

The letter ט is a sound produced by the teeth and the tip of the tongue. Rabbi Akiva, the great talmudic sage, says (in his work *Otiot d'Rabbi Akiva*, letter Tet) that the name of this letter should not be called טית (Tet), but טיט (Tit; the ט and ת are interchangeable, having similar sounds). טיט also means clay, material, plaster, or mortar. These are building materials used for making containers or coverings. Hence, the word בטח (*betach*, surety, strong faith), contains a ב (which stands for a house), a ט (for building material), and a ח (for life). Thus, בטח is the material that houses or shelters life, as we see in the songs of King David (Psalms, 115:9): ישראל בטח בה', עזרם ומגנם הוא; "Israel, trust in God, their help and their shield is he!"

The word טבה (*tova*, goodness) also contains a ט and a ב, being a vessel for goodness. These letters are all on the left side and represents the do of the first scale, the fa of the first scale, and the do of the second scale. The three letters preceding these three letters—ח, א, and ד (which are all on the right side)—spell the word אחד (*echad*, oneness), showing that unity is the basis for goodness.

The letter ע also represents a covering. When God created the first man, He bathed him in אור (*ohr*, light). When man sinned, He changed it into עור (*ohr*, a covering, a skin). The letter א, whose numerical value is 1, represents unity or oneness. The letter ע, whose numerical value is 70, represents expansion. There are seven Canaanite nations and seventy nations of the world, as well as seventy languages. There are seven colors of the rainbow, and seventy colors of the full spectrum. So, seventy represents something expanded, a whole gamut. The shape of the letter ע is that of two eyes which join and descend to the heart, which is affected by the eyes, with a nose in the middle. Notice how the words for "eye" in English, Russian (*oko*), and Spanish (*ojo*) all resemble two eyes and a nose. The word ע, עין, is *ayin* (eye). So we see that the letter ע is symbolic of the expansion one perceives with one's eyes.

Now we can understand the meaning of the word טבע (*teva*, nature) from its component letters. ט, the material; ב, which houses; ע, all that can be seen; i.e., the physical world as we see it.

CHAPTER 4

The Supernatural Scale

We have seen that all of the Hebrew letters correspond to a note in the first, second, or third scale, with the exception of the letter ת. This is because it represents the supernatural scale, which is above this physical world. Our Sages say that this letter signifies עולם הבא (*olam haba,* the world-to-come). The shape of the letter is that of the world with an opening at the bottom and one foot stepping out, or leaving this world for the next. The numerical value of ת is 400, which represents four dimensions, the fourth being a metaphysical incorporeal one. In this world, we perceive only three dimensions—length, width, and height—which are represented by the letter ש, which has three branches and numerically is 300. Those who merit reward in the world-to-come will no longer be limited by the dimensions of time and space. שבת (Shabbat), which is compared to עולם הבא (*olam haba,* the world-to-come) (Koheleth Rabbah, 1:36), is a word made up of two terms (שב–ת): שב (*shav,* return) to the ת (Tav), to the world-to-come—i.e. retrogress to the supernatural source, from whence we came.

It is interesting to note that the number of vibrations that make up the note *la* are 440, which is the numerical value of the letters ת (400) and מ (40) combined. These two letters form the Hebrew word תם (*tam,* perfect); the note *do* represents the perfection of all the notes, being the beginning and end of every scale.

Our Sages tell us that, since the ת represents a higher stage, in the world-to- come the musical key will contain more notes.

in the time of Moshiach (Messiah), the musical scale will contain an additional note, namely the ‫ה‬; at the time of the revival of the dead, an event that will occur after the advent of the Messiah, the scale will contain ten notes. Until that time, the ‫ה‬ can be considered a fourth scale on its own, denoting the otherworldly level of the world-to-come.

CHAPTER 5

The Reason for Four Scales

From Kabbalah, we know that there are four worlds: עולם העשי–ה (*olam haasiya,* the world of Action); עולם היצירה (*olam hayetzira,* the world of Formation); עולם הבריאה (*olam habria,* the world of Creation); and עולם האצילות (*olam haatzilut,* the world of Emanation). This idea can also be found in the order of the morning prayers as prescribed in the סדור (*siddur,* prayer book), tabulated by the אנשי כנסת הגדולה (*Anshei Kneset HaGedola,* the Men of the Great Assembly), the 120 Sages who led the Jewish people at the beginning of the Second Temple period. Included were such prophets as Ezra, Haggai, and Zachariah. These prayers progress in the same order as the order of the worlds. First, the morning blessings express man's physical needs and thank the Creator for their fulfillment. Next, the Pesukei d'Zimra (songs of praise) express the more emotional feelings of the heart. Third, the Shema (the declaration of God's unity), represents the devotion of the mind. Finally the Shemona Esrei represents the ultimate attachment to God himself. Hence, these four levels are a spiritual ascent, each stage a preparation for the next.

The spirit of man is also divided into four main categories. First, the נפש (*nefesh,* the physical spirit), which is concentrated in the liver and blood. Next, the רוח (*ruach*), a higher spirit located in the heart. Third, the נשמה (*neshama,* soul), in the mind. Last, the חיה (*chaya,* life spirit), and יחידה (*yechida,* individuality), are together outside the body and subsume the source of life. Going from octave to octave represents the spiritual elevation.

נגוני חסידות (*niggunei chassidut,* Chassidic songs) and even classical music are built of four parts. The first part usually represents feelings, emotions of the נפש, which is the spirit when it is still under secular or profane influence and is therefore very heavy. In the second part, one can feel the התעוררות (*hitorerut,* awakening) of the spirit. The third part is a feeling of happiness and joy. The fourth part is a feeling of attachment of the soul to higher sources and a higher level of awareness. Many famous melodies are composed this way, in an ascent of feelings.

CHAPTER 6

Elaboration of the First Scale

Do, the first note of the first scale, corresponds to the letter א. Ti, the last note of the first scale, is the letter ז. Together, these letters spell the word אז (*az*, then). When the word אז appears in the Torah, it refers to song—for example, in Exodus, (15:1): אז ישיר משה; "Then Moses sang." We can see that the word אז represents the scale from א to ז and the notes in between.

The word אז (*az*) also connotes God's sovereignty over nature. The letter א represents God for a number of reasons, as we shall see. The most obvious reason is that א is the first letter of the alphabet, and God is the first cause—the prime mover of Creation. The numerical value of א is 1, and T-d is the ultimate unity, as declared in the Torah (Deuteronomy, 6:4): ה' אחד; "God is one." The letter א also represents God's aspect of being אלוף של עולם (*Aluf shel olam*, Champion of the world). (Notice the similarity of the word אלוף, *aluf,* champion, and the English word "aloof," unapproachable.) The letter ז represents nature: Its numerical value is 7, and seven represents nature (seven colors of the rainbow, seven visible celestial bodies, seven days of Creation, seven days of the week). Hence, אז connotes God's mastery over nature.

At the splitting of the Red Sea, when the Jewish people sang the song of Moses (אז ישיר משה ובני ישראל), they saw clearly that every act of nature is subordinate to D-d's control. There are many levels of awareness of the extent of God's determination over his creation. Our Sages tell us that when a person is privileged to reach a high level of awareness in this area, he has a desire to sing. When the Jewish people's witnessed such a revelation by the Champion of Israel, they burst into song. According to Shimshon Raphael Hirsch, the word אז (*az,* then) is related to the word חז (*chaz*), which means "to see," as singing and seeing go together (see p. xx).

The letter א signifies a number of other important concepts. The א is made up of a slanted letter ו flanked by two י's. The numerical value of ו and two י's is 26 (ו = 6, י = 10, י = 10; 6 + 10 + 10 = 26). The number 26 is significant because it is the numerical value of God's most holy ineffable name, the tetragrammaton, י-ה-ו-ה (10 + 5 + 6 + 5 = 26).

The original shape of the א was not a י then a slanted ו and a י, as it appears today, but a י, a straight ו, and a י, or ייו. After Adam, the first man, sinned by defiling God's command and eating the fruit of the Tree of Knowledge, the letter took its present form. When a man sins, he becomes similar to the diminished א, which does not stand straight.

In Kabbalah, it is written that א represents the mind, ל the heart, and פ the mouth. The word פ, (פה, *peh*) means "mouth." These three letters spell the word אלף (*alef,* to learn). The letter ל and its mirror image depict a heart with its right and left chambers. Also, the ל is the middle of the alphabet, and the heart is in the middle of the body. A man understands an idea with his mind (א); the idea penetrates his heart (ל); and then the man is able to verbalize it (פ). The opposite of אלף (*alef,* learning), is the word spelled backwards, פלא (*peleh,* wonder), a lack of understanding. אלף (learning), therefore, represents harmony of these three parts of man.

By calculating the full numerical value of the word אז (*az*), different ideas are revealed. The full numerical value is obtained by adding together the value of the full name of each letter. The full name of the letter א is אלף (Aleph). Its value is 111 (1 + 30 + 80 = 111). The א therefore represents the unity of the ones, tens, and hundreds. The ones represents the solid earth; the tens, the liquid; and the hundreds, the gases. The higher the number, the higher the element. Hence, א contains the beginning of the three elements.

The full name of the letter ז is זיין (Zayin), so its full numerical value is 77 (7 + 10 + 10 + 50 = 77). This number stands for the perfection of the number seven. There are seventy nations of the world; seventy elders made up the Sanhedrin, the high rabbinical court prescribed by the Torah. The number seven represents the sphere of

מלכות (*malchut,* kingdom), and the seventh day, Shabbat. Thus, this number represents the perfection of nature. Seventy-seven is not only the *gematria* (numerical value) of זיין, which represents nature, but is also the *gematria* of the word מזל, (*mazal,* zodiac) (40 + 7 + 30 = 77). The zodiac, which refers to the stars, also refers to nature in general, and human nature in particular. We see clearly the relationship to nature between the letters א and ז.

When a person has a connection between the physical world and the spiritual world, he has a desire to sing. Singing is a result of the natural world (the number seven, the ז) joining with its higher root (the א). It is written in the book *Livnat HaSapir* (2 Kings, 3:15) that the reason that a baby is pacified when he is sung to is because the singing reminds him of the root of his נשמה (*neshama,* soul)— that is, the spiritual world from whence he came. When he remembers this world, he calms down. So, music and singing tie people to this spiritual source.

The א represents the כתר (*keter,* crown), the highest sphere and the source of all the spheres. כתר, in Kabbalah, is called פלא עליון (*peleh elyon,* the sublime wonder). The word פלא contains the same letters as the word אלף. In Kabbalah the crown is also called ארך אנפין (*erech anpin,* the long face). It is interesting to note that the numerical value of the word מוסיקה (*musika,* music; 40 + 6 + 60 + 10 + 100 + 5) is 221, which is the numerical value of the word ארך, the term used for the sphere of כתר. Even though מוסיקה is not actually a Hebrew word, our Sages also sometimes gave numerical values to foreign words. The reason is based on the principle that all languages are derived from and have a connection with Hebrew, the holy language. (For a deeper explanation, see my book *Hebrew: Source of Languages.*)

The prophets used music, song, and musical instruments to induce divine inspiration. אז (*az,* then), whose numerical value is 8 (1 + 7, שמנה, *shemona*) is the song of the soul (נשמה, *neshama*), as both words contain the same letters.

By adding together the full numerical value of the word אז (*az*), we obtain the number 188 (אלף = 111; זיין = 77; 111 + 77 = 188). The small *gematria* of this number is 17. This is obtained by adding together the digits (1 + 8 + 8 = 17). Seventeen is also the value of טוב (*tov,* goodness; 9 + 6 + 2 = 17). The numerical value of the letters א and ז are 1 and 7, respectively, which, when juxtaposed, form either 17 or 71. Seventeen is the same as the small *gematria*; 71 is the number of the members of the Sanhedrin, plus the נשיא (*nasi*, prince), head of the Sanhedrin, which represents a perfect cycle.

The numerical value of the word זבוב (*zvuv*, fly) is 17 (7 + 2 + 6 + 2 = 17). The fly represents impurity, which is the negative aspect of this number. The word זבוב is also related to the word זב (*zav*), which refers to someone afflicted with gonorrhea.

The Mishnah relates (פרקי אבות, *Ethics of the Fathers*, ch. 5, fourth Mishnah) that no fly was ever seen in the Beit Hamikdash (holy Temple) because of the קדושה (*kedusha*, holiness) of that place. This is indeed miraculous, as sacrifices were always taking place there. A remarkable occurrence once took place, in the yeshiva in Zichron Yaakov, concerning Rabbi Eliyahu Lopian זצ"ל (of blessed memory). It was the middle of the summer and a tremendous amount of flies were about, as was usual for that time of year. The *Rosh Yeshiva* (dean) was giving a lecture at midday, and he frequently had to stop because of the disturbance. He suddenly called the students' attention to Rabbi Eliyahu, who was sitting next to him. There was an area around Rabbi Eliyahu that the flies did not penetrate! The Gemara (*Berachot*, 10a) also relates that no fly ever came near the table of Elisha the prophet because of his great holiness.

In the Hebrew language, also known as לשון הקודש (*lashon hakodesh*, the holy tongue), one may obtain the essence of a word by determining its inner *gematria*. This is done by including only the interior letters of any word. For example, the inner *gematria* of the word אלף (Aleph) is לף, the value of which is 110 (30 + 80 = 110). The word זיין (Zayin), in turn, amounts to 70 (10 + 10 + 50 = 70). When we add these two values, we find that the inner *gematria* of the word אז (*az*, then) is 180. This is meaningful because this number is ten times חי (*chai*, life; 8 + 10 = 18; 18 × 10 = 180). This teaches that the word אז symbolizes the culmination of life, and that singing is an important part of a complete being.

Another example of inner *gematria* can be found in the letters ט, ב, and ח, which spell the word בטח (*betach*, security or faith). These are the only three letters in the alphabet whose inner letters of their full name is the same. The חית (Chet), בית (Bet), and טית (Tet) all have the inner letters ית (10 + 400), whose numerical value is 410, which is also the numerical value of the word קדוש (*kadosh*, holy; 100 + 4 + 6 + 300 = 410). This teaches that if a person wants to attain holiness, he must have strong inner security and faith.

CHAPTER 7

Elaboration of the
Second Scale

The second scale of seven notes consists of the letters ח, ט, י, כ, ל, מ, נ.
The ח represents חסד (*chesed*, lovingkindness); and חכמה (*chochma*,
wisdom). The י, like the ג of the first scale, corresponds to the divine
attribute of תפארת (*tiferet*, beauty), and is the collection of all things.
The כ represents חסד, kindness, which is the כתר (*keter*, crown), which
is closely related to the divine aspect of being כולו רחמים (*kulo
rachamim*, all-merciful). The ל stands for למוד (*limud*, learning) and
לב (*lev*, heart). The כ and ל spell the word כל (*kol*, everything) and קל
or קול (*kol*, voice; the כ and ק are interchangeable, having similar
sounds. We see, then, that voice is on par with totality.

Next we have the letter מ, which is equal to the attribute of יסוד
(*yesod*, foundation), which is symbolized by מים (*mayim*, water).
The letter מ (Mem) means water (מים, *mayim*). Water represents purity, which is the quality of the righteous. To continue, the נ represents חכמה (*chochma*, wisdom). The word נון (*nun*) means "to rule a
kingdom," which epitomizes *Moshiach* (see p. xx).

Each letter of the word מלך (*melech*, king) is built up with the
letters כ and ו (20 + 6), which together have the same numerical
value as God's name. The מ is a כ next to a ו; the ל is a ו on top of a
כ; and the ך is a כ with a ו beneath it. This teaches us that God is the
King of Kings.

We have seen that the first and last letters of a scale exemplify
the meaning of that scale as a whole. In the second scale, the first
and last letters are ח and נ, respectively. These letters spell the word

25

חן, grace. They are also the initials of the expression חכמת נסתר (*chochmat nistar,* hidden wisdom). The acquisition of חכמת נסתר is a high spiritual goal. The numerical value of נ is 50, which has several connotations. Fifty represents the metaphysical world, i.e., 7 (symbolic of nature) × 7 = 49. One above forty-nine is fifty, being above and beyond nature's realm. נ also represents the superlative level. There are fifty שערי בינה (*shaarei bina,* gates of understanding). The festival of שבועות, Shavuot, when the Jews received the Torah on Mount Sinai, was fifty days after the Exodus from Egypt on Passover. (Notice the similarity between the word נון, *nun,* and the English word "noon," which is the time of day when the sun is at its zenith). נ also represents the highest source, or root, of everything. Hence, the word נשמה (*neshama,* soul), is made up of two terms: נ-שמה ;נ, the root; שמה (*shama,* there).

The letter ח represents חיות (*chayut,* life). When placed after the נ, it spells the word נח (*nach,* rest). We see, then, that when the life force is in harmony with its spiritual root, it creates a situation conducive to tranquility.

CHAPTER 8

Elaboration of the Third Scale

The third scale consists of the letters ש, ר, ק, צ, פ, ע, ס. A veritable cornucopia of lofty concepts, this scale starts with the letter ס, shaped like a circle. The circle, as it is an unbroken shape, represents completion and fulfillment. It also represents infinity—having no beginning and no end. ס also stands for סומך (*somech*, support). King David said in Psalms (145:14): סומך ה' לכל הנופלים; "God supports the fallen." This divine quality is also mentioned in the Shemona Esrei prayer. As mentioned before, the ע represents the mouth. This is the medium through which man expresses speech, laughter, and song—characteristics that display man's superiority over animal. The צ denotes the צדיק (*tzaddik*, righteous man). ק stands for קדוש (*kadosh*, holy). The character of the letter ר is a ראש (*rosh*, head), which is the highest part of a man.

The final letter of the third scale is ש. It is said that God created fire, which is a source of light, with the letter ש. From this light, air and other things developed. (In English, many terms denoting light begin with the sound of the letter ש, such as "shine," "sheer," "shimmer," "chandelier."). The ש represents the beauty and harmony of light. In Hebrew, many words that betoken light and harmony begin with ש as well, such as שמש (*shemesh*, sun); שלום (*shalom*, peace); שאננות (*shaananut*, tranquility); שקט (*sheket*, quiet); שלוה (*shalva*, calmness); שבת (Shabbat, day of rest). The word שבת can be viewed as a phrase containing the two terms ש–בת. ש, harmony, of the בת

(*bat,* daughter of Israel). When a Jewish woman lights candles for the sabbath, she brings harmony into her household, which is her praise.

The שׁ also stands for שׁורשׁ (*shoresh,* root). The shape of the שׁ is like a root, and also like a שׁן (*shen,* tooth) with its roots. The word שׁורשׁ also contains two שׁ's.

The first and last letters of the third scale, which together summarize the significance of the scale as a whole, are the ס, the perfect circle, and the שׁ, the root of life. Together they represent the perfection of life. This idea can also be seen by their combined numerical value, which is 360 (שׁ = 300; ס = 60). As well, 360 is the number of degrees in a perfect circle; it is also the value of the word שׁין (Shin; 300 + 10 + 50 = 360), which is the full name of the letter שׁ. The small *gematria* of 360 is found by adding the digits together for a total of 9 (3 + 6 = 9). Nine, being the highest numeral, represents the superlative level. Nine also represents eternity, as any multiple of nine equals nine—e.g., 5 × 9 = 45 (4 + 5 = 9); 128 × 9 = 1152 (1 + 1 + 5 + 2 = 9); etc. No other number has these two qualities. Thus the third scale, in addition to being a stepping-stone from the rudimentary spiritual goals to the supernatural world (i.e., the fourth scale) is, in its own right, the realization of a medley of lofty ideals.

PART TWO

Musical
Terminology

CHAPTER 1

Introduction

We have seen that the spirit of a person consists of five parts: the נפש (*nefesh*), in the liver and blood; the רוח (*ruach*), in the heart; the נשמה (*neshama*), in the brain; and the חיה (*chaya*) and יחידה (*yechida*), outside the body (these being the aura, אורה, and halo, הלו; see Chapter 5, p. xx). These five parts correspond to five musical terms. The נפש (*nefesh*) is parallel to the term נגן (*niggun*), tune; the רוח to רנן (*raanan*), poetic song; the נשמה to שיר (*shir*), song; and the חיה to זמר (*zemer*), melody; and יחידה to קול (*kol*), voice.

The gradation of these musical processes develops in a specific order toward maturation. If a person מנגן (*menagen,* plays music), it means that he plays a plain, simple melody. When he is מרנן (*meranen*), he plays a higher type of music, more emotionally charged. When he is שר (*shar*, singing), this is even higher and more expressive, and the highest is מזמר (*mezamer*). The Malbim (Rabbi Meir Leibush ben Yechiel, 1809–1879, Chief Rabbi of Rumania and author of *Torah and Mitzvoth,* his profound commentary on the Torah) states that the זמר (*zemer*) is higher than the שיר (*shir*). שיר is a way of praising God for the wonders of the physical world he created, but זמר is a form of praise for the supernatural wonders of the universe. Let us turn to our holy writ for clarification. A quote from Psalms (105:2) states: שירו לו זמרו לו, שיחו בכל נפלאותיו. ; "Sing to Him, praise Him with music, meditate on all His wonders." This means that one starts with שירה (*shira,* singing), and progresses to זמה. This, in turn, leads one to שיחה (*sicha,* meditation on an upper plane), as seen in the order of these verbs in the verse.

In the song of Deborah (Judges, 5:3), it is written: אנכי להי אנכי, אשירה אזמר לה' א–לקי ישרא–ל; "I am for Hashem; I will sing and praise the God of Israel." Again, the progression is from שירה (*shira*) on the natural plane to זמרה (*zimra*) on the plane that is above nature.

The urge to dance accompanies musical pursuit, especially מנגן and שרה. Notice how the three letters of the Hebrew alphabet that precede the three letters of the word שרה (*sharah*) are רקד (*rakad,* dancing). This shows a close relationship.

The word רקד (*rakad*) also means "to sieve," indicating that dancing has the power to purify and cleanse the soul of man. The word רקד is built up from רק–ד (*raik* Dalet); "the emptying of the ד," the four elements. It is interesting to note that dancing, in the secular world, emphasizes the bottom part of the body (the physical aspect), while in religious dancing, it is the upper part of the body (corresponding to the soul) that is emphasized. This shows how Judaism stresses the spiritual aspects of life, whereas in the secular world the physical is always stressed.

When one proceeds to מרנן (*meranen*), his heart is full of joy and lively spirit, an uplifting of the רוח (*ruach*).

When going on to שר (*shar*), the נשמה (*neshama*), situated in the mind, is enlightened. When advancing to מזמר (*mezamer*), one feels full of life, which is applicable to the חיה (*chaya*), which means life-force.

When we examine the relationship between these words, a beautiful idea is revealed. Taking the word זמר (*zemer*), one sees that its first letter, ז, represents מלכות (*malchut,* kingdom) and is positioned in the middle (see chart, p. xx). The מ, the second letter, represents יסוד (*yesod,* foundation) in the second octave, and is also in the middle; the ר, the third and final letter, is also יסוד in the third octave, and likewise also is in the middle. Hence, all the letters of the word זמר have their counterparts positioned in the middle.

The word שיר (*shir,* song) has an identical pattern. The ש—its first letter, like the ז of זמר (*zemer*)—represents מלכות (*malchut,* kingdom), as both are seventh in their appropriate scales and are also interchangeable, having similar sounds (both are dental letters). The י, its second letter, which represents תפארת (*tiferet,* beauty), and its third letter, ר, which corresponds to יסוד (*yesod,* foundation), are also in the middle. Thus, שיר also consists of three parts, all focused in the middle.

The word רנן (*ranen*) consists of a ר, positioned in the middle, as seen in זמר (*zemer*) and שיר (*shir*), and a נ, which is seventh in the second scale and so is parallel to מלכות (*malchut,* kingdom) in the middle. Our Sages tell us that one of the names of the Messiah is ינון (*yinon*) because the נ (נון) represents מלכות, and the Messiah will be king.

The word נגן (*nagen*) consists of the letters נ and ג, both being in middle positions.

The significance of the middle position is that it represents balance. It is like a fantastic puzzle to see how all the letters of all these musical words fall neatly into positions that mean balance. We see that music has the power to elevate a person above the physical level and place him in a state of perfect spiritual equilibrium. Hence, music puts a person in a state in which he can sing. Many forms of Jewish meditation can be used to elevate a person's consciousness of God, but the potency of music, as indicated by its expressions and inferences, makes it an invaluable and precious instrument in the devout believer's orchestra.

CHAPTER 2

The Simple Tune

The letters of the word נגן (*nagen*) are also the initials of the words נפש (*nefesh*), גוף (*guf,* body), and נשמה (*neshama*), which shows that the נגון (*niggun*) affects these three aspects of a man. נגן (*nagen*) is also a combination of the letters נ and ג, which correspond to the divine attributes of מלכות (*malchut,* kingdom) and תפארת (*tiferet,* beauty), respectively. שבת (Shabbat) is also a combination of these two attributes, as it represents מלכות, God's rule over the world, and תפארת, beauty and harmony. It is a great form of divine worship to sing songs on the Sabbath. Indeed, many great rabbis have written tunes and lyrics for Shabbat songs, and most סדורים (*siddurim,* prayer books) contain a variety of these lyrics. For example, "Yom Zeh L'Yisrael" was written by Rabbi Isaac Luria (better known as the Arizal) (1534–1572), who is considered by many to be the greatest kabbalist who ever lived. "Ki Eshmerah Shabbat" was written by Abraham Ibn Ezra (1080–1164), who, in addition to being a talmudic scholar, was an expert in grammar, mathematics, Jewish philosophy, astronomy, and medicine. He wrote an important commentary on the Torah, and was an accomplished poet as well.

A small handful of Hebrew words read the same backward and forward; one of them is the word נגן (*nagen*). This teaches that music is "contagious"—i.e., one tune brings another in its wake. Music stimulates a person to sing again and again. When one is involved in composing, he can compose one song after another in a kind of melodic momentum.

A similar idea is related to the word נתן (*natan*), giving, which is also a palindrome. If one gives with a full heart, then one has the need to continue giving. Furthermore, real giving is as much receiving as it is giving.

The name of King David, דוד, also reads the same backward and forward. The name דוד, David, represents humility, as ד stands for דל (*dal*, poor). In the book of Psalms, King David frequently mentions his lowly status; for example (Psalms 22:7): ואנכי תולעת ולא איש; "And I am a worm and not a man." King David—the most righteous man in 2,900 years! The humbler he was, the more he strove for humility; and the closer he came to perfection, the more remarkable and valuable was his humility.

In contrast, we find an extremely haughty force in the world referred to in Scripture as גוג ומגוג, *Gog um'Gog*. גוג is also a palindrome. The letter ג stands for גאוה (*gaava*, pride), and גמל (*gamal*, high). Hence, Gog is the force that embodies conceit, vanity, insolence, and condescension.

The נ of נגון (*niggun*) represents understanding. As we have seen, there are fifty (נ = 50) levels of understanding. As we have seen, נ stands for גמל (*gamal*, high, in this context meaning uplifted), and for גדול (*gidul*, growth), and גבוה (*gavoa*, grand). So, נגון (*niggun*) signifies a growth of understanding. Music helps one to meditate, to think deeply, to understand more. בינה (*bina*, understanding) is the root of strength and glory. בינה and חסד (*chesed*, lovingkindness) are positioned on the left; חכמה (*chochma*, wisdom) is on the right. The Levites represent גבורה (*gevura*, strength), on the left. The Levites were descendants of Levi, son of our Patriarch Jacob. The tribe of Levi was chosen, because of its great piety and erudition, to serve in the Beit Hamikdash (holy Temple). Part of their daily service was to play musical instruments and sing. Within the Levites were כהנים (Kohanim), those Levites who were descended from Aaron, who was himself a Levite. The Kohanim performed special services in the Temple, including sacrificial offerings, and the Kohen Gadol (the High Priest), on Yom Kippur (the Day of Atonement), was able to enter the קודש קודשים (*kodesh kedoshim*, the Holy of Holies) to offer special forms of worship. Aaron himself was Kohen Gadol. The Kohanim represent חסד, situated on the left.

To understand the connection between the aforementioned concepts and how they relate to נגן (*nagen*), let us turn to the תקוני זוהר (*Tikunei Zohar*), the *Zohar* (the book of splendor). The word נגן

is made up of two terms: נ–גן, the letter נ (Nun) and the word גן (gan, garden). The Zohar says that the definitive garden, the Garden of Eden, appertains to strength. So, the נגון is a link between the Garden of Eden and strength, representing גבורה (gevurah, strength) and בינה (bina, understanding). If we take the word גן and replace its first letter, ג, with the letter that follows it, ד, we have the word דן (dan, judgment). The connection between שיר (shir, song) and דין (din, judgment) can be seen by rearranging the letters of the word שיר spelled in full: שין, יוד, and ריש, which, rearranged, spell יש דין יושר: "There is straight judgment." This shows a close connection. To replace the ג of גן with the ג's preceding letter, ב, we spell the word בן (ben), which is the root of the word בינה.

The two letters following the letters of גן are דס, which is at the root of the word סוד (sod, secret). In Kabbalah it is stated that גן (gan) is a concept that is connected with סוד, which means that a melody (גן is the inner concept of נגן) can elevate a person to the point where he transcends the mundane and reaches the sphere of סודות (sodot), knowledge hidden from normal man under normal circumstances.

The word סוד (sod) is also related to the planet נוגה (Noga, Venus), second from the sun. The three letters following its root letters, נגה, are סדו (ו–ה, ד–ג, ס–נ) which spell the word סוד. The word נגה also means brilliance and glory. Hence, after the level of illumination and brilliance is the attainment of secret knowledge. One of the methods used by sorcerers, alchemists, and magicians was to invoke this planet and attempt to obtain impure powers by making contact with it.

The *gematria* of נגן (nagen; 50 + 3 + 50) is 103. When we remove the zero, a non-value digit in this context, we are left with 13, a number that represents unity for several reasons. Thirteen is the *gematria* of אחד (echad, one; 1 + 8 + 4 = 13). By adding together the digits we obtain the small *gematria* of 4 (1 + 0 + 3 = 4; 1 + 3 = 4). There are four letters in the ineffable name of God, י–ה–ו–ה, which is the paragon of unity. Four also represents unity, as there are four elements that together make up the world: fire, water, air, and earth.

Indeed, music has the power not only to unify people, but also to break down the psychological and social barriers between people. We see in the book of Joshua (ch. 6) that Joshua commanded that the shofars (ram's horns) be blown in order to make the walls of the city collapse. We also see that, at a Jewish wedding, families come together to dance and sing. The men and women dance separately, for the sake of modesty and purity. By singing and dancing, they are also doing the *mitzvah* of gladdening the bride and groom. So, by joining together to sing and dance, the barriers between them fall away, and they are united in joy and holiness through the medium of music. What better way to create a relationship between two families than to unite in spiritual joy and harmony?

The *gematria* of נגן (*nagen*), 103, is also the *gematria* of the word מְנֻחָה (*menucha,* rest; 40 + 50 + 8 + 5 = 103). (When the ו acts as a vowel, it can be grammatically replaced by a dot over the previous letter, and therefore has no numerical value.) It is also the value of מנחה (Mincha). מנחה is the second of the three daily prayers prescribed by our Sages. It corresponds to the מנחה (meal offering) brought in the Beit Hamikdash (the Temple). The Mincha prayer is considered the most serious and desirable of the three daily prayers, as it is in the middle of the day, and a man must break his daily routine to say it. The other prayers are said only in the morning (Shacharit) or at night (Maariv). Ideally, a man should always be involved in prayer, but by prescribing mandatory prayers at fixed times of the day, the whole Jewish nation has an opportunity to join together to beseech the Holy One for peace and prosperity for the Jews and for the world. This national unity makes these prayers very valuable. In many communities, it is the custom on the Sabbath to sing some of these beautiful prayers, such as "Aleinu," "Adon Olam," and "Lecha Dodi." So, we see there is a connection between נגן, מנוחה, and מנחה. A man must be settled, at rest, especially in order to pray. When Elijah the prophet prayed to God to destroy the four hundred false prophets of Baal (1 Kings, 18:19), he was answered at the Mincha prayer.

The first two letters of the word מנחה (Mincha), i.e., מן (*man*), mean strength. Man (מן), in English, is a גבר (*gever*), which is derived from the word גבורה (*gevurah,* strength). This same idea can be found in the name Haman (המן) and other words. Hence, the letters מן are letters of strength. Now we can understand why the Mincha service has such power. מנחה also has the same letters as the word נחמה (*nechama,* comfort). Music also has the ability to comfort people, especially children.

The numerical value of נגן is the same as that of the word עגל (*aigel,* calf; 70 + 3 + 30 = 103). This is the negative aspect of the number. עגל refers to the Golden Calf mentioned in Exodus (32:19).

When misusing music, which is a powerful force, one has the negative impetus of idolatry, which is symbolized by the Golden Calf. Contemporary pop music is steeped in wickedness, as is often indicated by the names of the groups or their songs.

The message is clear: We must remove all impure influences and non-Jewish infiltration from our lives and return to the sublime, Torah-true Judaism. Only then will our spiritual and physical enemies will be rendered powerless.

On the positive side, a word with the same consonants as עגל (aigel) is עגול (agol, circular), which also has a gematria of 103 (when the ו is ignored). When a stone is tossed into water, it produces circles; music has a similar ripple effect. When music is played in spiritual purity, it induces the desire to continue, and one melody brings another in its wake. In a similar vein, our Sages say that one mitzvah brings another in its wake, and that the reward of a mitzvah is a mitzvah—i.e., the immediate opportunity to do another mitzvah (Ethics of Our Fathers, 4:2).

The Hebrew language has the quality of being able to reveal information through "keys." One of these "keys" is called the key of א"ת ב"ש. The letter א, the first letter of the alphabet, is interchangeable with the letter ת, the last letter; the ב, the second letter, is interchangeable with the ש, the second-to-last letter; and so on. In the key of א"ת ב"ש, the word נגן (nagen) equals טרט. These are the letters of the word רטט (ratat, vibration). רטט represents the shaking, or metabolism, of the physical body. The root of the word נגן is גנן (ganen), to defend. Thus, music has the power to defend the spirit from the physical clutches of the profane. The word רטט also shows that music shakes up the physical to reveal the spiritual. The numerical value of רטט is 218. (200 + 9 + 9 = 218). The number 218 is also the value of the word ריח, scent, which refers to the spirit of a person, the רוח. This concept is indicated in the Havdalah prayer, said on Motzei Shabbat (Saturday night) at the departure of the Sabbath. Fragrant spices are smelled, and the pleasant scent appeases and compensates one for the loss of the extra expanded soul (נשמה יתרה, neshama yetaira) received on the Sabbath, which will return the following Sabbath (Abudraham). Hence, נגן and its counterpart רטט indicate another aspect of music's positive potential that is waiting to be utilized.

The full gematria of the word נגן (nagen) is 285. (נון, גמל, נון; 50 + 6 + 50, + 3 + 40 + 30, + 50 + 6 + 50 = 285). The number 285 is significant for several reasons: 285 is the value of the word רפה (*rafa*, to relax; 200 + 80 + 5 = 285). It is also the value of the word פרה (*para*, cow). (Notice the similarity between the word "heifer" in English, and הפרה—*hapara*, the heifer—in Hebrew.) The word פרה refers to the פרה אדומה (*para aduma*, the red heifer) mentioned in Scripture (Numbers, 19). The red heifer is frequently mentioned in the *Zohar*. The פר (*par*, bull) represents power and strength. The *gematria* of פר is 280, which is ten times twenty-eight. Twenty-eight is the numerical value of the word כח, strength (20 + 8 = 28). Multiplying the number by ten signifies fullness (here, full strength). This concept is revealed on Hoshana Rabba. On Hoshana Rabba (the Day of Great Salvation), which falls on the seventh day of the *Sukkot* holiday, a bundle of five ערבות (*aravot*, willow branches) is struck upon the ground.

As well, 280 is the value of the sum of those letters of the Hebrew alphabet that have "final" counterparts, meaning that when they are placed at the end of a word their form changes slightly (ך = 20, ם = 40, ן = 50, ף = 80, ץ = 90; 20 + 40 + 50 + 80 + 90 = 280). The final letters close off the word, setting the word's limit and therefore symbolizing the quality of strength. When we add the כולל (an additional value added corresponding to the number of letters in the word—in this case the value of 5, one for each letter), we arrive at the number 285, which is the full *gematria* of the word נגן (*nagen*). Consequently, strong connections are revealed between the נגן and the ideas of strength and power.

The second letter of נגן (*nagen*), the ג, is the third letter of the alphabet and represents תפארת (*tiferet*, beauty). If we retain the letter ג and substitute the letters נ in נגן for the letter ה, we get the word הגה (*hege*, meditation). (ה may be substituted for נ since the small *gematria* of נ is 5; נ = 50 = 5 + 0 = 5.) In the daily Maariv (evening) prayer we declare the words: יבהם נהגה יומם ולילה; "We will meditate on them (the words of the Torah) by day and night." This is in line with God's teaching to Joshua that God will grant success to the Jews if the words of Torah are observed and are meditated on (Joshua, 1:8): והגית בו יומם ולילה; "And meditate on them day and night."

If we substitute the letter ג for the letter ב—the letter that precedes it in the alphabet—we go from the letters נגן to נבן. The three letters are at the root of the word להתבונן (*lehitbonen*, to consider or meditate).

If we write out the full name of the letters of the word נגן (*nagen*; נון, גמל, נון) and then take the inner *gematria* of these letters, we arrive at the number 182. (ון, ון, מל; 6 + 50, + 40 + 30, + 6 + 50 = 182.) It is no coincidence that this number is also the *gematria* of יעקב (Jacob, our father; 10 + 70 + 100 + 2 = 182.) Jacob stands for תפארת (*tiferet*), as is indicated by: תפארת ליעקב; "beauty for Jacob." Jacob represents the perfect balance between right and left, between Abraham (חסד, *chesed,* lovingkindness) and Isaac (גבורה, *gevurah,* strength).

By rearranging the digits of the number 182, we get 218. The number 218 is the value of the word ריח (*raiach,* scent; 200 + 10 + 8), representing the nose, which is in the middle of the face and again denotes balance and equilibrium. Or, we can arrange the digits to 281, which is the value of the word פאר (*p'er,* to beautify; 80 + 1 + 200 = 281).

When a tune is played properly, it has the power to beautify a person by uplifting his spirit, and to beautify the world around him.

CHAPTER 3

Harmony, Beauty, and Power

The quality of harmony is closely related to the sphere תפארת (*tiferet*, beauty), which is appropriately positioned in the middle of our kabalistic tree. The root of the word תפארת comes from the word פארות (*pe'erot*, branches). The divine attribute of תפארת is at a central location, and the other attributes branch off from it. תפארת is also related to פאר (*p'er*, to beautify, glorify). The letters ר, א, פ can be rearranged to form many different words, such as פרא (*pere*, wild); אפר (*afar*, ashes); and רפא (*rafo*, healing). Let us examine the relationship between these words and the concepts they represent.

The Arizal discusses the meaning of the word רפא (*rafo*, healing). When someone is sick, he is in a פרא (*pere*, wild situation); his faculties are no longer under his control. At this point he is obligated to call a doctor, רופא. The word רפא is made up of two terms: רף–א. רף (*raf*) loosens the א, which represents the mind—i.e., he helps him shake loose of the sickness which is adversely influencing him, and returns him to his proper plane of balance, to the פאר (*p'er*, beauty) of a properly functioning body.

The word אפר (*afar*, ashes) refers to the ashes of the פרה אדומה (*para aduma*, the red heifer). It was a *mitzvah* to use the ashes of the red heifer, burnt on the altar in the Beit Hamikdash, to purify a person who was טמא (*tameh*, impure) so that he could enter the Temple. In Jewish thought, certain objects render impure the one who touches them. There are various levels of impurity, and remedies for each. The highest level of impurity is contact with a dead body (טמאת מת, *tumat met*). The vacuum created by the loss of a man created in God's image is filled by the most powerful forces of impurity. The only remedy for this condition, prescribed by the Torah, is the ashes of the red heifer. Once purified, all who come in contact with the deceased, such as those who were involved in the *mitzvah* of burying him, may enter the Beit Hamikdash again. Ashes have a purifying effect: They draw any foul entity toward them. The ashes are themselves a vacuum (caused by the burning of the red heifer). The heifer is consumed, and the ashes left in its place draw in the impurity through the process of spiritual cohesion. The impurity of the person who comes into contact with the ashes is drawn into the ashes, leaving him pure and in a state of פאר, harmony. Ashes also symbolize purity by virtue of their material worthlessness, equated with the quality of humility. Humility is an essential ingredient in the recipe for a spiritually pure life.

We have seen that the word פאר (*p'er,* to beautify) is at the root of the word תפארת (*tiferet,* beauty). The *gematria* of פאר is 281, which, when rearranged, is 182, which is the inner *gematria* of נגן (*nagen*) and the numerical value of יעקב, Jacob. Jacob represents תפארת, and the numerical value of his name (182) is also equal to seven times twenty-six. Twenty-six is the value of God's name, the tetragrammaton, and seven is the number of notes in the musical scale: do, re, mi, etc. Joseph is 6 × 26, Jacob is 7 × 26, and Isaac is 8 × 26.

$$יוסף = 10 + 6 + 60 + 80 = 156 = 6 \times 26$$
$$יעקב = 10 + 70 + 100 + 2 = 182 = 7 \times 26$$
$$יצחק = 10 + 90 + 8 + 100 = 208 = 8 \times 26$$

Thus, we see that Jacob, whose attribute is תפארת, is closely related to the perfection of the musical scale and to the perfection of God's name.

As mentioned before, the nose is the center of the face, representing balance and harmony. Jacob embodies these qualities, as indicated by his close connection with the sense of smell. When Jacob came to receive the eternal blessing from his father, Isaac, Isaac stated (Genesis, 127:27): ראה ריח בני כריח שדה אשר ברכו ה'; "See, the fragrance of my son is like the perfume of a field blessed by God." Rashi says that this referred to the smell of the Garden of Eden (Genesis, 27). This also suggests that תפארת (*tiferet,* beauty) as ריח (*raiach,* smell) is 218, which, rearranged, is 281—which is the value of יעקב (Jacob) and פאר (*p'er*), both of which stand for תפארת.

According to Kabbalah, the letter א has the power to balance forces. In the word פאר (*p'er*), the א divides the letters פר (*par*), which by themselves mean "bull," and represent power. In this case, the א indicates that harmony is the result of the balance of powerful forces.

The three letters preceding the three letters of the word פאר (*p'er*) are עתק (*atak*), which means far and lofty (the ת, the last letter of the alphabet, is counted as preceding the א, the first letter, since the Hebrew language is infinite, like a circle). The עתק is the name of a כתר (*keter*, crown), which, on our kabbalistic tree, is positioned in the middle and above תפארת (*tiferet*, beauty) in the middle. Thus, we see how תפארת and its root word stand for balance, strength, and harmony.

CHAPTER 4

The Poetic Song

The term רנן (*ranen*) is seen a number of times in the Psalms of King David. In the first verse of Psalm 95 the author declares: לכו נרננה לה' נריעה לצור ישענו; "Come, let us give song to God; let us call to the Rock of our salvations." This verse is the opening exultation of the קבלת שבת, inauguration of the Sabbath prayer. Psalm 100 proclaims (v. 2): באו לפניו ברננה; "Come before Him with song!" The fact that רנן is a higher form of song than נגן (*nagen*) can be seen by their letters. Both have the two נ's, but רנן has the ר, the value of which is 200, and נגן has the ג, with a value of 3. The ר and ג are interchangeable, according to the א"ת ב"ש code, but ר is a three-digit number, being in the hundreds, and is on a higher level than three, a one-digit numeral.

The letters רנן (*ranen*) are the initials of the words רוח (*ruach*); נפש (*nefesh*); נשמה (*neshama*). These parts of the spirit of man are parallel to the heart, body, and liver of man. The רנן has the power to elevate the physical and enlighten the mind, and, thus, has an effect on all three.

The letter ר stands for ראש (*rosh*, head), which is the location of the mind. ראש also means beginning, as in ראש השנה (*Rosh Hashana*), Head of the Year—i.e., new year. The letter נ represents understanding. The double נ in רנן (*ranen*) is for emphasis. Thus, together, these letters imply the beginning of deep understanding.

CHAPTER 5

The Meaning of Song

The word שִׁיר (*shir,* song) is the noun of the verb שָׁר (*shar,* sing), which has the same letters as the word שַׂר (*sar,* minister). A שַׂר is a person with power, one who has control over others. One is only worthy of a position of power when he has control of himself. Joseph was placed in a position of power in Egypt because he was able to control himself with Potiphar's wife. When a person reaches the level of שַׂר (minister) and can control himself, then he can שָׁר (sing). The sole duty of the מלאכי השרת (*malachei hasharet,* the heavenly ministers) is שירה לה׳; "singing to God."

Another word related to שָׁר (*shar,* sing) is אשור (*ashur,* perceive). When Bilaam prophetically saw the future of the Jewish nation, he said to Balak (Numbers, 24:17): אראנו ולא עתה, אשורנו ולא קרוב; "I perceive it (the nation of Israel), but not in the immediate future." אשור has the same root as לשיר (*lashir,* to sing). The letter י, which represents the future, is the middle letter of the word שיר (*shir,* song), and therefore can be read שׁר-י, which means "seeing the י, the future." This shows why the song (שיר) is used for prophecy—seeing into the future.

That singing has the power of farsightedness can be seen, according to Rabbi Shimshon Raphael Hirsch, in the introductory word אז (*az,* then) of the Song of the Sea, which is related to the word חז (א and ח being interchangeable, as guttural letters), which is the root of the word חזה (*chazo,* seeing; see p. xx). שור (*shur*) means deep insight, great foresight. So, when a man sees clear miracles, he is able to sing. If he gains control over his body, mastery over his physical being, he can understand and see into the future, having released himself of the physical blinders of this world. This constitutes a high level of prophecy. If he cannot gain control, he remains confined. Hence, singing is a result of self-control.

The letters of the word שׁר (*shar*) reveal additional interesting thoughts. The שׁ represents the beauty and harmony of light; the ר stands for ראשׁ (*rosh,* head). Therefore, שׁר (singing) is on par with a bright shining of the mind. We also learn from this that when a man understands something clearly, or resolves a problem and releases himself from doubt, he sings. The *gematria* of שׁר is 500 (300 + 200 = 500). This represents the perfection of the number five.

The number five is significant for a number of reasons. There are five senses: sight, sound, touch, taste, and smell. There are five parts to the spirit. The world was created with the letter ה, which numerically equals five, and, hence, this number represents Creation. Five multiplied by ten is fifty, which represents the fifty gates of understanding and the fifty levels of purity. This is an even higher level than five, for understanding and purity are a consequence elevating the five senses, the five parts of the spirit, and the Creation, bringing them to fruition. Subsequently, five hundred represents a very high level, and a highly elevated state.

שׁירה (*shira,* song) is one of the ten names for prayer (תְּפִלָה, *tefilla*). The numerical value of שׁירה (300 + 10 + 200 + 5 = 515) is the same as that of תפלה (400 + 80 + 30 + 5 = 515). The inner numerical value of the word שׁירה (*shira,* song) is 385 (שׁין, יוד, ריש, הה: הה, ין, וד, יש, ה = 10 + 50, + 6 + 4, + 10 + 300, + 5 = 385), which is the same as the numerical value of the word שׁכינה (*Shechina,* the divine Presence; 300 + 20 + 10 + 50 + 5 = 385). Thus, the letters שׁ and ר teach us that singing can elevate a person to a high spiritual level.

The letters of the word שׁיר (*shir,* song) can be rearranged to form a number of words that relate closely to song. The word ישׁר (*yashar*), for example, means straight or honest. If a person is straight and honest, he can sing and find joy: ולישרי לב שׂמחה; "Happy are the straight and upright" (Psalms, 97:11). The letters of the word ישׁר (*yashar,* straight), according to the key of א"ת ב"שׁ (שׁ = ר; ב = י; י = מ) = ג) is equal to 45. This is the same numerical value as the word אדם (*adam,* man; 1 + 4 + 40), which shows that man was created straight, as is written (Ecclesiastes, 7:19): אשׁר עשׂה את האדם ישׁר; "As He created man straight." Another word having the same letters is רישׁ

(Resh), the letter ר. The character of the letter ר is ראש (*rosh,* head), as in ראש גלות (*rosh galuta,* head of the community in exile). In Jewish thought, ריש represents ענוה (*anava,* humility). This is because a רש (*rash,* poor man) can become the best שר (*sar*). The רש is always in a rush, having to earn enough money for his next meal.

The letter ר connotes movement. In English, words like race, raise, rambler, rover, roam, rapid, reel, and roll imply movement and begin with the "rrr" sound, which sounds like a motor racing. In Hebrew, words like רץ (*ratz,* race), רגל (*regel,* foot), רוח (*ruach,* wind), רחש (*rachash,* to move), רכב (*rechev,* vehicle), רכיבה (*rechiva,* riding), רעידה (*reida,* shaking), and רקד (*rikud,* dance) also denote movement. Thus we see that the רש (*rash,* pauper), will move to being ראש (*rosh,* head). Sometimes the person who seems the lowest is actually the highest in the eyes of God, and vice versa. History bears this out. All too frequently, the kings and rulers have been cruel, evil, and corrupt, while the poor but honest citizens have suffered harsh decrees or even martyrdom at the hands of these despots. In the world-to-come, each will receive his due.

Thus, we see that ר is equal to head and to humility, hinting at the fact that in the world of truth there will be a movement of each to his proper place. In music, a parallel concept is hinted at by the note do. This note can be the highest or lowest, depending upon its octave. When one is on a very low spiritual level, he has the potential to rise to the very highest realms of spirituality.

The Modzitzer Rebbe, in his discourses about the musical scale, wrote that when a person goes down and down, he gets very close to the beginning. This is what is meant by what has been said about our generation. The more a generation deteriorates, the more it will be able to awaken and arise. We may be farther away from the Creation of the world, or the revelation at Sinai, but we are closer to the coming of the Messiah than ever before, and are moving closer all the time. Albert Einstein, the eminent Jewish physicist, said that if a spaceship took off from earth and traveled in a perfectly straight path, after almost an eternity it would return to its starting point, not unlike an insect walking along a globe: At any given moment is appears to be moving forward, but soon it is walking toward the place where it began. One who has the holy Torah as his guide can transcend the dimensions of time and space and realize his proper place.

In the musical scale, as one descends toward the do, he is simultaneously approaching the highest note of the previous scale.

This is reminiscent of the adage (Proverbs, 24:16): שבע יפול צדיק וקם;
"The righteous may fall seven times, but he will rise." From the bottom there is no place to go but up. Hence, the easiest time to influence people is when they are low and feeling down. Once they are on the rise, they begin to feel as if they know everything.

Another interesting explanation of why the word ריש (*raish*) has·the same letters as שיר (*shir*) is that by singing, one touches the source (head, beginning) of one's soul. The letters of the word שיר (*shir,* song)—ש, י, ר—represent בינה (*bina,* understanding), חכמה (*chochma,* wisdom) and ראש (*rosh,* head), respectively. Hence, שיר touches the head, which represents wisdom and understanding, which is the source of everything in the world.

The numerical value of שיר (*shir*) is 510 (300 + 10 + 200 = 510). The small *gematria* is 6 (5 + 1 + 0 = 6). Six is parallel to the sphere of יסוד (*yesod*). If we take the small *gematria* of each letter of the word שיר, we also arrive at 6 (300 + 10 + 200 = 3 + 2 + 1 = 6). These three numbers also allude to the shapes of the letters of the word itself. The ש is three branches; the י is one small line; the ר is two lines. The number series 3, 1, 2, arranged in ascending order, is 1, 2, 3, which corresponds to the do, re, mi of the musical scale. Hence the foundation of music can be found in the word שיר.

The number series 1, 2, 3 reappears in the *gematria* of the word ענג (*oneg,* enjoyment; 70 + 50 + 3 = 123). This is the same numerical value as the word הנגינה (5 + 50 + 3 + 10 + 50 + 5; *hanegina,* the music). This also shows that music is a great source of enjoyment. If we replace the ג of ענג with its subsequent letter, ד, we obtain the letters of the word עדן (Eden), which is symbolic of true happiness.

The letters preceding the word שיר (*shir*) are רטק, which form the word קטר, which is similar to כתר (*keter,* crown); the ק and כ, and the ט and ת, are interchangeable, as each pair sounds alike. When letters or words are close together, it shows that there is a close relationship between their meanings—for example, the subsequent letters of the א and מ, which together form the word אם (*eim,* mother), or ב and נ which spell בן (*ben,* son). Obviously, a mother and son have a close relationship, as Jewish law states that "the son goes after the mother"—i.e., whatever religion the mother is, so is the son.

Since כתר (*keter*) is at the top of our kabbalistic tree, it shows how important singing is, and that through singing one may attain a very high spiritual level.

The numerical value of כתר (*keter*) is 620 (20 + 400 + 200 = 620). The number 620 represents the *mitzvot* because there are the 613 *mitzvot* of the Torah, plus seven. Seven is the number of *mitzvot* given to the children of Noah (i.e., the non-Jews, since all the nations of the world are descended from Noah and his sons), and seven is also the number of rabbinic *mitzvot*. The *mitzvot* of the children of Noah are:

1. Do not murder.
2. Do not steal.
3. Do not have illicit sexual relationships.
4. Do not swear falsely using God's name.
5. Do not worship idols.
6. Do not tear the limb off an animal and eat it.
7. Enforce these laws with courts and officers.

The seven rabbinic *mitzvot* are:

1. Laws pertaining to Purim.
2. Laws pertaining to Chanukah.
3. Lighting candles prior to Shabbat and Yomim Tovim (holidays).
4. *Netilat yadaim* (washing hands before eating bread).
5. *Eruv tavshilin* (preparing food on Thursday for Shabbat when Friday is a festival).
6. *Eruv chatzerut* (coordination of the dwellers of a building with a common courtyard to allow them to carry from home to home).
7. Blessings recited before partaking of food or performing *mitzvot*, etc.

Thus, כתר (*keter*, crown) is synonymous with the full cycle of *mitzvot*, the penultimate way of worshipping God.

The small *gematria* of 620 is 8 (6 + 2 + 0 = 8), which represents the supernatural world. Hence, שיר (*shir*) can open the gates of heaven, which cannot be opened by other means. There are certain עולמות (*olamot,* worlds) that can be penetrated only by music. The *Zohar* states that the היכל הנגינה (*haichal hanegina,* palace of music) is closely related to תשובה (*teshuva,* repentance). Thus, the prophets were able to use music to awaken their inspiration and cling to God.

The letters preceding the ש, י, and ר are ר, ט, and ק, which also form the word קטר, *keter*); ק may be exchanged with כ, and ט with ת,

as each pair sounds the same). The root of the word כתור is כתר (*keter*, crown). כתור is also linked to the word קשור (*kashur*, connected). (The ת and ש are close, as can be seen in Aramaic grammar, where the Hebrew ש is a ת in Aramaic (e.g., "snow" in Hebrew is שלג, *sheleg,* and in Aramaic is תלג, *teleg.* The Aramaic language is so close to the holy tongue that it is called "the dress.") Thus, the offering in the Temple of קטורת (*ketoret,* incense) was a means of connection, a tying together of the upper and lower worlds. On Yom Kippur the High Priest would offer incense to elevate and connect this world to the higher world, and gain atonement for the sins of the Jewish people. שיר (*shir*) serves the same purpose: to unite the upper spheres, embodied in כתר, with our own world.

CHAPTER 6

The Melody

We have seen that the זמר (*zemer*) is parallel to the נשמה (*neshama*), which is the highest part of the spirit within man. זמר (*zemer*) is the highest level of song. The word לזמר (*lezamer,* to play music), also means to shear or shave. This is because music helps a person to cut off the קליפות (*klipot,* shells) that conceal the spirit. Just as a nut has a shell that must be broken and removed to reveal its fruit, so the spirit is concealed by all the mundane distractions of the physical world. People are tricked into thinking that it is more important to read newspapers or to see a movie than to pray or learn Torah. But when someone has an uplifting spiritual song and he joins in and sings, he is rejuvenated ("re-Jew-venated"), and can joyfully worship his Creator. So זמר helps cut away the קליפות that cover the spirit. The נשמה, which is situated in the heart, is covered by קליפות, which can be reached through זמירות (*zemirot*).

We have seen that the numbers 1, 2, and 3 represent the do, re, mi of the musical scale, and also represent the word שיר (*shir*). The numerical value of זמר (*zemer*) is 247 (7 + 40 + 200 = 247), which divided in half is 123 1/2. This shows us that זמר is on a higher level than שיר. In Kabbalah, the numbers 6 and 7 can be considered equal: The seventh sphere, מלכות (*malchut*), is a collection of the other six, and the seventh heavenly body, the earth, is the focal point of the other six. Similarly, when mixing paints, one can mix the six colors (the three primaries—blue, red, and yellow—and the three secondaries—green, orange, and purple) to obtain black. This is the mystical reason behind the custom of wearing black clothes on the Sabbath.

The numerical value of the word זמר (*zemer,* 247, plus the *kollel,* i.e., 1 for the word itself) is 248, which is identical to the number of positive commandments. This teaches us that singing brings man to fulfill the commandments through the awareness of his soul.

By examining the letters of the word זמר (*zemer*), a wealth of information unfolds to us. The letter מ is actually a combination of the letters כ and ו. When separated, in זמר, we are left with the word זכור (*zachor,* remember). Singing helps one to remember, especially by putting the words of something to music (e.g., Mishnayot) and then singing it. It is customary to sing זמירות (*zemirot*) on the Sabbath, and the Torah states (Exodus, 20:8): זכור את יום השבת לקדשו; "Remember the Sabbath day to keep it holy." Many scientific tests have been done to determine to what extent music aids memory. These tests concluded that music is a highly potent mnemonic device. In the brain, the right hemisphere controls sight, and the left hemisphere controls speech. By combining the two sides, i.e., combining something one sees (right side) with music (left side), a person can remember much better because much more of the brain is being used to recollect this piece of information. Thus, the words זכור (memory) and רכוז (*rikuz,* concentrate) have the same letters, for concentration helps memory. The word זכר (*zachor,* remember), is made up of two terms: זך (*zach,* pure) and ר (Resh, head). When one's mind is pure and void of distractions, one can remember properly.

The three letters of the alphabet that follow the three letters of זמר (*zemer*) are ח, נ, and ש. These spell either חשן (*choshen*) or נחש (*nachash*). חשן refers to the חשן משפט (*choshen mishpat,* breastplate of judgment) worn by the כהן גדול (*kohen gadol,* High Priest) (Exodus, 28:15): ועשית חשו משפט; "Make a breastplate of judgment." In contrast, the word נחש, snake, refers to the negative aspect of these letters, while חשן refers to the positive. Let us examine them further.

The letter ח and ז represent the supernal world; the ח has a value of 8, one above 7, which is symbolic of nature. The נ equals 50, one above seven times seven. Thus, the letters close to זמר represent spiritual depth and brightness.

One may ask why the letter ש, synonymous with light, appears in the word שקר (*sheker,* falseness). The letters קר denote cruelty, which can even be seen in such English words as cruel, crime, crucify, critical, cross, crook, and cry, and in Hebrew words קר (*kar,* cold); קְרָב (kerav, fight); קֻרְבָּן (korban, victimize); קִרְקֻר (kirkur, destroy). Hence, קָר signifies negative ideas. The biblical sinner and enemy of Moses, our teacher, was קֹרַח, Korach (Numbers, 16). His name consists of קָר and ח, which stands for חֵטְא (chet, sin). Korach is the epitome of a sinner, and as such he was punished through supernatural means, as it says (Numbers, 26:10): "The earth opened its mouth and swallowed the rebellious group and Korach."

So, the letters קָר belong in the word שֶׁקֶר (sheker), yet ש, symbolic of light, appears in it too. Actually, for a lie to have any chance of being believed, it must have some grain of truth (the ש) in it; the bit of truth gives the lie the validity it needs to be believed. Thus, we see that when Moses sent twelve spies to examine the land of Israel before the Jews entered it (Numbers, 13:1), they lost their faith in God and returned to the Israelite camp with a bad report of the land. Instead of saying merely that the land was bad, or that the inhabitants were too powerful to conquer, however, they first reported that the land was "indeed flowing with milk and honey" (ibid., 13:27); only then did they add that the natives were "giants" and "aggressive," and that the land ate up its inhabitants (ibid., 13: 28, 32). When the nation heard this report, they believed it! Thus, they and the spies were punished for not trusting God; they were not permitted to enter the land, and the nation of Israel had to wait until a whole new generation was born, forty years later, before entering. Together with Joshua, they then easily conquered and took possession of the holy land.

The words נָחָשׁ (nachash) and חֹשֶׁן (choshen) are diametrically opposed, חֹשֶׁן representing the positive side and נָחָשׁ, the negative. In חֹשֶׁן, the ח stands for חַיִּים (chayim, life); the ש for light; and the נ for depth of understanding. The חֹשֶׁן מִשְׁפָּט (choshen mishpat, breastplate) that the High Priest wore was full of light, and the stones that it contained actually glowed in response to the High Priest's requests. The ח also stands for חֶסֶד (chesed, lovingkindness), which either can be a great mitzvah and a useful tool to bring people to God, or can be misused and lead to lust. Self-indulgence, gluttony, adultery, homosexuality, euthanasia, exoneration of criminals, and lust are examples of misplaced mercy. Abraham represented pure and proper חֶסֶד, and he fathered the righteous Isaac, who represented גְּבוּרָה (gevurah, strength). Ishmael, on the other hand, absorbed only negative qualities, and as a result became the epitome of lust. The Mishnah in Ethics of Our Fathers mentions those people who can be compared to a sieve and those who are like a strainer. The sieve filters out the lumps, bugs, and stones, and retains the fine flour; the strainer lets the fine wine pass through, and retains the useless dregs.

In the word נחש (*nachash,* snake), the נ denotes the fifty gates of impurity, the ח stands for חטא (*chet,* sin), and the ש stands for שן (*shen,* tooth), which is used to consume and destroy. In this light we can understand a related Midrash. The name of the snake contains letters that describe its main characteristics. It stands for sin (ח), having caused the first man's sin; and it contains impurity (נ)—i.e., poison—between its teeth (ש). Furthermore, if we exchange the letter ח in נחש with its following letter, ט, we obtain the letters of the word שטן (Satan). The snake is symbolic of the Satan, whose job it is to tempt man to sin. Man must strive to conquer this inclination and attain holiness.

There are numerous examples of great musicians and composers who became very corrupt, many of whom even died from sicknesses caused by the טומאה (*tumah,* impurity) of an evil lifestyle. Music elevates a person to such a high level that one must have some meaningful form of expression to direct one's energy. If a person does not have a positive way of expressing himself after playing or hearing music, he feels an awful emptiness, which leads him to seek something to fill the void. When confronted with an attractive sin at such a moment, it is very hard to resist, and thus, evil and lust may fill the vacuum. The Germans constantly listened to the music of great composers and attended operas and symphonies; they were then charged up to direct their Godless energies to mass murder and other evil deeds. Many recent pop stars have led corrupt lifestyles and died very young.

At particular periods in time, the gates of Heaven opened up, bringing down spiritual abundance that influenced the world. Accordingly, the great surge of classical music occurred at the same time as the development of the Chassidic movement. The Baal Shem Tov (Rabbi Yisrael), the founder of the Chassidic movement, lived at the same time as Johann Sebastian Bach; the Baal HaTanya (Rabbi Shneur Zalman of Liadi, founder of the Chabad movement) lived at the same time as Mozart and Beethoven; and Rabbi Nachman of Breslav lived at the same time as Franz Schubert. The *Zohar* said that the gates of science would open 5,600 years after Creation. At that time, the Industrial Revolution (1840, corresponding to the Jewish year 5600) took place, and the Oral Torah and *yeshivot* flourished as a consequence. This shows that the source of wisdom and music is divine.

When Rabbi Levi Yitzchak of Berdichev, a great *tzaddik* of the eighteenth century, saw that music was becoming an overly powerful and dangerous force, he prayed for God to "close the tap" to so much inspiration in music. This explains why the classical music movement came to a sudden close, and the level of music has never reached the same plane.

So we see by the letters following זמר (*zemer*) that song is a powerful tool which, like anything in the world, can be used for good or evil, for a blessing or a curse. The Torah commands that we use the goodness of the world for a blessing, as we see in the book of Deuteronomy (30:19): "I have placed before you life and death, the blessing and the curse . . . . Choose life, so that you and your descendants will survive." The proper way of life for a Jew is prescribed in the Torah: how to be holy; how one should dress, eat, speak, and act to obtain holiness. In this way he will rid himself of confusion and be set free. For example, the prohibition against eating certain foods, and the strict sexual laws, lead one to self-control and make one master of his instincts rather than a slave to them. Indeed, the prophets were men who used the Torah to attain great wisdom. They used music to attain prophecy and helped lead the masses to repentance. The root of the word נבואה (*nevua*, prophecy) is נבא, which is actually made up of two terms: נ, the fiftieth gate of understanding, and בא (*ba*, comes). Today we have great rabbis to lead our generation; all we need to do is to ask their advice and follow their example.

זמר (*zemer*) has the same letters as the words זרם (*zerem*, current) and רמז (*remez*, hint). Music sends currents through the body, motivating a person to move and act. There are "hints," indications, that there is something deeper beyond what is visible. In Hebrew, words relating to music indicate many deep concepts, as we have shown. One need only open his eyes and ears, for the answers are all there, even before the questions have been asked.

CHAPTER 7

Praise for the Natural and Miraculous

The Master of the Universe is to be praised for the wonders he performs in both the physical world and the spiritual world. Both worlds are infinitely complex and great, and testify to God's unfathomable wisdom. We are able to perceive with our senses the orderliness of the universe; the complicated biosystems that exist in each climate and topography on earth; chemical and biochemical laws; atomic structure; physiology; etc. The laws of nature, gravity, electromagnetism, and quantum mechanics do not change. One may notice that in any system, be it as simple as a garden or as complex as a lunar space station, there is a tendency toward entropy, chaos, and disorder. Energy must constantly be put into a system to maintain it. Thus, the laws of the universe and the orderliness of the world testify to their Maker, without whom all would fall into disarray.

Mark the words of the wise King Solomon (Proverbs, 24:30): "I passed the field of a lazy man and it was overgrown with weeds, and I beheld, I put my heart to it, I took instruction." The supernal world is also infinitely complex. Souls, spirits, spheres, angels, and so on exist simultaneously with the physical world, yet remain unseen. Although one cannot perceive these metaphysical creations under normal circumstances, they, like God himself, can be felt indirectly; we can feel their effects. Similarly, even though we cannot see an atomic particle, we can feel its effects. After experiencing a nuclear explosion, no one would deny the existence of an atomic particle or the basics of being unable to see one. Therefore, an atomic particle is somewhere in the twilight zone between the physical and spiritual worlds.

The more spiritual and less physical a person becomes, the closer he gets to understanding God, and the higher becomes his eternal position in the world-to-come. The Torah stresses the importance of the Jew's involvement with spiritual matters (Deuteronomy, 28:9): "If only you will keep the *mitzvot* of Hashem your God and walk in his paths, God will establish you as his holy nation, as he promised you. All the nations of the world will realize that God's name is associated with you, and they will be in awe of you." Also note Exodus (19:5): "Now if you obey Me and keep My covenant, you shall be My special treasure among all nations because all the world is Mine. You shall be a kingdom of priests and a holy nation to Me."

In the Psalms, sometimes the word שיר (*shir*) is used; sometimes מזמור (*mizmor*) is used, as in Psalm 29 (v. 1); and sometimes both, as in Psalm 23 (v. 1): מזמור לדוד ה׳ רעי לא אחסר—"A song of David. God is my shepherd, I shall not lack." Sometimes the word שיר is used, as in Psalm 133 (v. 1): שיר המעלות לדוד. הנה מה טוב ומה נעים שבת אחים גם יחד—"A song of ascent of David. Behold! How good and pleasant it is when brothers dwell together in unity." Sometimes both terms are used together, as in Psalm 92 (v. 1): מזמור שיר ליום השבת טוב להודות לה׳ ולזמר לשמך עליון—"A song of the Sabbath day. It is good to thank Hashem and to sing praise to your name, o exalted One." The Malbim says that this is because שיר represents happiness and praise of God for the natural world, and מזמור refers to the supernatural world.

Many people are able to see God's influence in the natural world. Our Sages tell us that if a person works to see God and to understand him through nature, then God will show him true miracles. Many people have felt supernatural influences or have seen inexplicable incidents in their lives. There are numerous accounts of rabbis who were privileged to see great miracles. The more clearly a person knows that everything is a miracle, the more manifest miracles God will show him. An unbeliever does not have the merit to be shown a miracle, for he has hidden God from himself, and himself from God. Furthermore, the Holy One blessed mankind with free will and the ability to do good or evil, so that one may choose good and gain merit. If God were to reveal himself to an atheist, this would remove his free will. Thus, a man who already knows that the Master of the World rules all will not lose anything when confronted with clear divine influence. To such a man, "miraculous" events are no more miraculous than the birth of a baby or the rising of the sun. Who, however, would not feel an exalted thrill at being given the gift of witnessing a miracle? We understand God through his actions. Thus, if a person tries to see God in the world, sometimes he is blessed with a more manifest action and the chance to see God even more clearly. There are numerous accounts of reliable eyewitness testimony that supernatural occurrences took place.

Now we are able to understand the verse in Psalms (105:2): שירו לו, זמרו לו—"Sing to Him, make song for Him!" One starts with שיר (shir), praise for the natural miracles that occur every moment, and then one may proceed to זמר (zemer), praise for the supernatural miracles.

However, at times God shows open miracles, and then it is clear that all of Creation is a miracle. This is seen in the concept of Shabbat. When one keeps and guards the Sabbath, he reaches a higher spiritual awareness, which he carries with him into the week, achieving a weekly renewal. As we have seen, שבת (Shabbat) is שב (shav, return), to the ת, to the supernal source, the supernatural scale.

So, Shabbat, the seventh day, gives one the feeling that the world has more to offer than physicality. All over the world, a week is seven days long. Why has the week been seven days long in all times and all places? The world was created in seven days, and the seven-day week has been an unbroken tradition of mankind since the first man. God rested (שבת, rest) on the seventh day—not because the Omnipotent One was tired, but as a lesson to man to refrain from the mundane one day a week, carrying the holiness with him into the week. We can understand the order מזמור שיר ליום השבת (Psalms, 92:1), i.e., praise for the miraculous, praise for the seemingly natural. Thus, depending upon his spiritual needs, a person may first be inspired by the supernatural, leading him to praise the natural, or vice versa. Some psalms start off with מזמור לדוד, "a song of David", and some start off לדוד מזמור, "of David, a song." מזמור לדוד means that King David first needed to start playing music to lead and inspire himself to bring out his soul. Sometimes, however, he was inspired without outside stimuli, and was able to immediately start playing his harp with divine inspiration, to recite and compose psalms. This is when מזמור לדוד is used.

This same idea can be found in the order of the words נבל (*nevel*, lyre) and כנור (*kinor*, harp). The נבל, which is connected to the attribute of חכמה (*chochma*, wisdom), is on a higher plane than that of the כנור, being connected with the attribute of בינה (*bina*, understanding). When the נבל precedes the כנור, as in the verse (Psalms, 57:9 and 108:3): עורה הנבל וכנור; "Áwaken the *nevel* and *kinor*," wisdom precedes the understanding, showing that there is first an awakening from above (similar to the idea of מזמור לדוד). When the כנור (בינה, understanding) precedes the נבל (חכמה, wisdom), the awakening is from below (see the idea of לדוד מזמור), as can be seen in the verses (Psalms, 81:3): כנור נעים עם נבל; "A pleasant *kinor* with a *nevel*" and (Psalms, 33:2): הודו לה' בכנור, בנבל עשור זמרו לו, "Thank Hashem with a *kinor*, with a *nevel* of ten strings sing to him."

Using musical instruments to arouse awakening from below can be further seen in Psalms (149:3): הללו שמו במחול ותוף וכינור-י יזמרו לו; "They will praise His name with dance, with a drum and a harp they will sing to him." The order of the musical instruments in this verse is parallel to the ascending attributes. The מחול (*machol*, dance) is parallel to the sphere of גבורה (*gevurah*, strength); the תוף (*toph*, drum), to חסד (*chesed*, lovingkindness); and the כנור (*kinor*, harp), to בינה (*bina*, understanding). These three attributes are in ascending order from the bottom up, once again showing that prophecy is awakened from below.

CHAPTER 8

Song and Eternity

ספירת העומר (Sefirat haOmer, the counting of the days between Passover and Shavuot) is forty-nine days long. On each day of the Omer, Psalm 67, containing forty-nine words, is recited. The four words related to song are contained in the introduction to this psalm (1:1): למנצח בנגינות מזמור שיר; "For the Conductor upon melodies, a tune, a song," and in the psalm itself (v. 4) it is stated: ישמחו וירננו לאמים; "The nations will be glad and sing for joy." (The Radak says that נגינות, *neginot,* here refers to a type of musical instrument.) The four expressions for song represent the four parts of the נפש (*nefesh*). The number 49 represents unity, as its small *gematria* is the same as the *gematria* of אחד (*echad,* one; 1 + 8 + 4 = 13, 4 + 9 = 13). Each word of the Psalm 67 and each day of the Omer bring one closer to unity.

The words נצח (*netzach,* eternity) and פסח (Pesach), also have a small *gematria* of 13. נצח (50 + 90 + 8 = 148) and פסח (80 + 60 + 8 = 148) also equal each other (1 + 4 + 8 = 13). This is because the Jewish people achieved eternity and unity through Passover. Together with זמר (*zemer;* 7 + 40 + 200 = 247), which has a small *gematria* of 13, we arrive at 39 (3 × 13 = 39). Thirty-nine is the value of טל (9 + 30 = 39). טל (*tal*) stands for the supernal crown, as in טליר טל אורות; "Yours is a crown of light." There are thirty-nine מלאכות (*melachot*), principal categories of skilled labor that were used in the building of the Mishkan and that are forbidden on the Sabbath. On Shabbat there are thirty-nine (טל) lights, which shine on our נשמה (*neshama*).

(Note the similarity between the number 39 and לט. לט means a "covering," having the same letters as the word טל, and the English word "light.") When one of the thirty-nine מלאכות is done on Shabbat (God forbid), the light cannot shine on the נשמה.

CHAPTER 9

The Uniqueness of Voice

The קול (*kol,* voice) represents the fifth and highest part of the soul, the יחידה (*yechida*), which is unique to each individual. The three letters following the word קול are מ, ז, and ר, which spell זמר. One starts with the קול, and then uses and develops it to make זמר (*zemer,* song). In that sense, the קול is the potential and the זמר is the realized.

Kabbalah describes how the shapes of the letters for the word קול (*kol*) represent its meaning. We start with ק, which has a stem that touches the lowest point in the alphabet. Next comes the ו, which is exactly in the middle. Finally comes the ל, which touches the highest point of any letter. This shows that a person can ascend higher and higher letters using his voice for song and prayer. The Hebrew word for ladder, סולם (*sulam;* 60 + 6 + 30 + 40 = 136), a tool used to go up, has the same numerical value as קול (100 + 6 + 30 = 136). Furthermore, the letters of God's name, י–ה–ו–ה, describe how the sound of the קול is produced. The letter י represents the depth of sound that comes from the inside of man and triggers the respiratory process. The five parts of the respiratory system are symbolized by the letter ה, which has a value of 5. The five parts are the two lungs (one on the left, one on the right), and the two bronchial tubes, which unite to form the trachea (windpipe).

The next step is expiration of air through the throat. This is denoted in the letter ו, which looks like the throat with its opening at the mouth and connection to the windpipe. Finally, the letter ה again represents the sounds leaving the mouth through the five parts of the respiratory system. The letter ה has a *gematria* of five, and the five types of sound are gutturals (אחה"ע), produced by the throat; the labials, (בומ"פ) produced by the lips; the palatals (גכי"ק), produced in the palate; the letters [or dentals] (דטלנ"ת) produced by the tip of the tongue against the front of the palate; and the sibilants (זשר"ץ), produced by expelling air from between the tongue and the teeth. The repeated number five is reminiscent of the five parts of the spirit.

We can see that the production of sound through the mouth to produce words, a process that is too often taken for granted, is described by the letters of God's name. The production of words and the processes of singing and speaking, functions that set man above the animals, are intrinsically spiritual. The Talmud Yerushalmi asks why, since man has two ears, two eyes, two nostrils, etc., he was not created with two mouths; indeed, one mouth to be used for holy functions, and the other to be used for the secular. The Talmud concludes by saying that, unfortunately, man speaks too much nonsense, gossip, and profanity with one mouth; imagine what would happen if he had two.

The Mishnah (*Ethics of Our Fathers,* 5:1) says that God created the world by uttering words. The first word of the Torah, בראשית; "In the beginning," starts the account of Creation. This word contains the five types of sounds mentioned before. ב is a labial letter, ר is a sibilant, א is a guttural, ש is a sibilant, י is a palatal, and ת is a dental. So, all of the groups are represented in the first word of Creation. The five sounds also parallel the Five Books of Moses.

As we have seen, the *gematria* of קול (*kol*) is 136. From the numerals themselves, we learn an interesting lesson.

ק	= 100	= א	= 1	= do	=		חסד
ו			= 6	= la	=		יסוד
ל	= 30	= ג	= 3	= me	=		תפארת

From here we see the importance of קול, that it is the source of everything, since these are the main spheres. These numerals are the same as those in the number 613, which is the number of *mitzvot* in the Torah. Adding these numerals together, we get the number 10 (6 + 1 + 3 = 10). Ten represents totality and completeness, as there are ten spheres, ten fingers and toes, ten statements by which the world was created, and Ten Commandments at the revelation of Sinai. This is one of the reasons why prayers should be said with a congregation of at least ten. Note the similarity between the words עשר (*eser,* ten) and עושר (*osher,* wealth). The Mishnah teaches (*Ethics of Our Fathers,* 4:1): "Who is wealthy (עשיר, *ashir*)? The one who is happy with what he has."

As already mentioned, קול (*kol*) is parallel to the fifth part of the spirit, the יחידה (*yechida,* uniqueness). The ultimate unity is God himself, so we see that קול is the foundation of everything. The small *gematria* of יחידה (10 + 8 + 10 + 4 + 5 = 37; 3 + 7 = 10) is 10, and the small *gematria* of ten is 1, the unity (1 + 0 = 1). When one teaches Torah to another person, he is transmitting the word of God. In that sense, there is a voice within the voice. קול within a קול can be seen by the remarkable process of taking the full value of the word and then adding the inner *gematria*. The full value of קול is למד; וו; קוף. Now, the inner letters are וף (6 + 80); ו (6); and מד (40 + 4, taken by removing the first letter). The value of the inner letters is then 136 (68 + 6 + 44 = 136). The number 136 is also the *gematria* of the word קול, as we have seen (100 + 6 + 30 = 136). Thus, we have a graphic account of the voice within the voice. Indeed, the more one sings, the more one gets out of singing. Often, the one playing or singing music experiences a higher surge of fervor than his audience.

The word ממון (*mamon,* money) also teaches a lesson when we examine the inner letters of the full value. The full value is: מם; מם; וו; נן. Notice how the inner letters of each letter are the same as the outer letters. This shows that the more money one has, the more one wants. "Money is inside money"—that is, money produces a desire for more money. As King Solomon said (Ecclesiastes, 5:9): "The lover of money is not satisfied with money."

We can see that the קול has deep connections with such concepts as the foundation of Creation, the unity of God, completeness, and the divinity of the Torah. By avoiding improper speech and by voicing holy words and songs, one can connect to some of the highest spiritual planes.

CHAPTER 10

Expressions of Joy

In Jewish tradition, a bride and groom are given seven special blessings from honored guests on their wedding day and on the seven festive meals that make up in the celebration. In the seventh blessing, seven expressions of joy are bestowed on the newlyweds. First, ten terms are listed, the first six being expressions of joy and the last four being the result of joy. These ten terms are parallel to the ten wedding canopies that God created for Adam and Eve in the Garden of Eden (*Baba Batra,* 75). Later in the blessing, a seventh expression of joy is used. We have the terms ששון (*sasson,* joy); שמחה (*simcha,* happiness); גילה (*gila,* mirth); רינה (*rina,* glad song); דיצה (*ditza,* pleasure); חדוה (*chedva,* delight); then, later, is צהלות (*tzahalot,* jubilance). The expressions denoting the result of joy are אהבה (*ahava,* love); אחוה (*achva,* brotherhood); שלום (*shalom,* peace); and רעות (*reiut,* companionship).

The seven terms denoting joy correspond to the seven מידות (*midot,* divine attributes):

chedva	חדוה	lovingkindness	חסד
ditza	דיצה	strength	גבורה
rina	רינה	beauty	תפארת
gila	גילה	eternity	נצח
simcha	שמחה	glory	הוד
sasson	ששון	foundation	יסוד
tzalah	צהלה	kingdom	מלכות

Let us examine some of their relationships.

שמחה (*simcha*) is parallel to הוד (*hod*, glory), which is the fifth attribute. The word שמח (*sameach,* happy) is built up of the letters ש–מח, "the shininess (ש) of the brain (מח)," which shows that happiness is a result of, and also causes, enlightenment of the "brain," of thought. The inner *gematria* of the word שמח, whose letters are שין, מם, and חית (ית + מ + ין = 10 + 50, + 40, + 10 + 400 = 510), is the same as that of the words שיר (*shir*, song) and ישר (*yashar*, straight, honest; 10 + 200 + 300 = 510). This shows that happiness contains honesty and the ability to see the truth, i.e., being "straight."

According to the key of א״ל ב״ם, the word שמח (*sameach,* happy) is the same as יבק (Yabok), a name that is connected with Jacob, as the Torah says (Genesis, 32:23): "Jacob passed over the bridge of Yabok." Mystically, this means that Jacob achieved a deep spiritual level, as is indicated by the numerical value of the letters יבק (10 + 2 + 100 = 112), which are equal to the three names of God: ה־י־ה־א;י־ו־ה־ה;א־ד־נ־י (1 + 5 + 10 + 5, + 10 + 5 + 6 + 5, + 1 + 4 + 50 + 10 = 112). These three names correspond to the three middle spheres of the ten spheres. א־ה־י־ה corresponds to the highest sphere of the כתר (*keter*, crown); י־ה־ו־ה to תפארת (*tiferet*, harmony); and א־ד־נ־י to מלכות (*malchut*, kingdom), showing that these three attributes function as the center channel to bring down the divine influences, which is achieved by being שמח. Our rabbis tell us: אין השכינה שורה אלא מתוך שמחה; "The divine glory rests only where there is joy." The numerical value 112 is also the same as the two names of God that represent judgment and mercy—א־לקים, which relates to God's attribute of judgment (86); and י־ה־ו־ה, relating to mercy (26)—which, added together, equal 112. שמח has the power to bring harmony between the two extremes of judgment and mercy. A similar phenomenon can be found in the letters ש and מ of שמח, which represent, according to the *Book of Formation* (related to our forefather Abraham), to the fire (ש) and water (מ). By being שמח, a man can bring harmony between these two opposing forces in his life, which is the ח (חיות, *chayut*, life). Jacob is distinguished with the attribute of שמחה (*simcha*, happiness), as is written (Psalms, 14:7 and 53:7): יגל יעקב ישמח ישרא–ל; "Jacob will rejoice, and Israel will be glad." According to the key of א״ל ב״ם, the letters of יעקב correspond to the letters of שמחה.

The letters of the word שמחה (*simcha*) are the same as the number חמשה (*chamisha*, five). Similarly, the expression ששון (*sasson*, joy) is related to the number six (שש, *shesh*), which has to do with the sixth attribute of יסוד (*yesod*, foundation) representing purity. (It is interesting to note that when one tunes a musical instrument one tunes it to the sixth note, la, which in C major is the note "a," the first letter of the alphabet. This idea points to the foundation, the יסוד, being the sixth attribute.)

The number seven (שבע, *sheva*) is related to the word שבע (*savea*, satisfied), indicating that when a man reaches the seventh attribute, which is kingdom, he feels satisfied with life. The number eight (שמנה, *shemona*) in Hebrew contains the same letters as the word השמן (*hashmen*, fattening), indicating that there is an additional stage above the normal, which is represented by this number. The letters are also the same as those of נשמה (*neshama*, soul). From this we see that the spheres are the roots of the physical and emotional world.

גילה (*gila*, joy) is parallel to the quality of נצח (*netzach*, eternity), which represents Moses and Aaron. The word גילוי (*gilui*, revelation) comes from the word גילה. נצח is closely related to the word צח (*tzach*, bright). The letter נ represents the superlative level. Thus, נצח means נ–צח, the highest brightness when all is revealed. When a man is confused and then the truth is revealed to him, he is happy. This type of happiness is called גילה (*gila*) because the truth was revealed (גילוי) to him.

רינה (*rina*) corresponds to the attribute of תפארת (*tiferet*, beauty) and also represents unity in music. The small *gematria* of רינה (*rina*) is 13 (200 + 10 + 50 + 5 = 265; 2 + 6 + 5 = 13). Thirteen, we have seen, is the *gematria* of אחד (*echad*, unity). We see that thirteen represents balance and perfection, which is the quality of תפארת. The balanced scale consists of thirteen semitones parallel to the thirteen attributes of God mentioned in the Torah (Exodus, 34:6).

The word דיצה (*ditza*), corresponds to גבורה (*gevurah*, strength) and is close to the word צדי (*tzadi*), צדקות (*tzidkut*, righteousness). צדיק (*tzaddik*, righteous person) has its root in the word צד (*tzad*, hunter). The character of the letter צ is a fish trap. The צדיק is one who hunts and traps his evil inclination. Mystically, the letter ק represents the evil inclination. One reason for this is that the full name of the letter ק is קוף (Kof), which is spelled the same as the word קוף (*kof*, ape). An ape, the יצר הרע (*yetzer hara*, evil inclination) tries to "ape," or copy (קופי, similar to קוף), holiness. Without the divine gifts that make man unique—i.e., speech, a higher soul than animals,

etc.—man would be an ape, and those people that have not elevated themselves by controlling their animal tendencies are less than
apes. (Some people have even stated that they believe themselves to
be descended from apes. Incredible!) One may ask, "Why is the letter ק foremost in the word קדוש (*kadosh,* holy) if it symbolizes the
evil inclination?" The word קדוש is made up of two terms: ק (the evil
inclination) and דש (*dash,* to thrash or destroy). A holy person is one
who has destroyed his evil inclination.

קדוש (*kadosh,* holy person) is on a higher level than צדיק (*tzaddik,* righteous person). The צדיק is still hunting the last bits of his evil
inclination, but the קדוש has destroyed it. The word קוף (Kof) comes
from the word הקף (*hekef,* surrounding), as the evil inclination sur-
rounds one at all times. The word יצר (*yetzer,* inclination), has the
same letters as the word ציר (*tzayar,* painter). The letters ר and ד are
sometimes interchangeable, as they have similar shapes. Hence the
יצר (evil inclination) works by painting a seemingly pleasant picture
(ציר, *tziyur*) and then springing a trap (ציד, *tziyed*). The negative aspect of the hunter is embodied in Esau, whom the Torah refers to as
איש ידע ציד; "a skilled trapper" (Genesis, 25:27). Esau was trapped by
his own evil inclination, and mentor, to trap others.

חדוה (*chedva*) is parallel to the attribute of חסד (*chesed,* lovingkindness), and represents perfection. This can be demonstrated
by viewing the word חדוה as two terms: חד—וה. חד (*chad*) means
unity, as in חד גדי-ה (*chad gadya*); "one baby goat" (Passover Haggadah). ו—ה are the last two letters in God's name, י-ה-ו-ה, and represent the seven divine attributes, ו being the first six (ו = 6) and ה
representing מלכות (*malchut*). The remaining expressions in the seventh blessing are אהבה (*ahava*), אחוה (*achva*), שלום (*shalom*), and
רקות (*reut*), which are results of joy, as mentioned earlier. The *Zohar*
says that אהבה (love) goes together with יראה (*yira,* fear). Where
there is no fear of God, there can be no love of him, and where there
is no love, there can be no fear. The רבון כל העולמים (Ribon Kol Ha-
Olamim), a prayer read on Shabbat, says, תן בנו יצר טוב לעבדך באמת
וביראה ובאהבה; "Give us a virtuous desire to worship You with honesty, fear, and love." This lovely prayer has been set to music and is
frequently heard in *yeshivot* at festival times, most notably Simchat
Torah.

The *Shla HaKadosh* says that when there is too much fear, then
one may come to spill blood (God forbid), since one needs a balance of fear and love. These qualities are related to the attributes of

חכמה (*chochma,* wisdom) and בינה (*bina,* understanding), since part of love is חכמה and part of fear is בינה. This is why a husband and wife balance each other, the husband representing אהבה (*ahava*) and חכמה and the wife representing יראה (*yira*) and בינה.

Just as a person ascends the musical scale of notes, each one parallel to a higher divine attribute, a person may ascend higher and higher levels of joy.

PART THREE

The Musical
Instruments

CHAPTER 1

Introduction

Clearly, music, melody, and harmonic sounds have the ability to move and uplift human emotions. They are invaluable tools in man's never-ending quest to praise and laud his Maker. King David himself played seventy musical instruments, and his Psalm 150 (קן) mentions nine of them, each representing a division in a system of classification relating to the kabbalistic spheres, as well as a category of those human emotions used by man to stir and free his soul to extol God, and help him to fulfill his spiritual potential and purpose.

Hashem is to be acclaimed, the psalmist tells us, with the following musical instruments, and he lists them in the following order:

1. *Shofar* (שופר, ram's horn)
2. *Nevel* (נבל, lute)
3. *Kinor* (כנור, harp)
4. *Toph* (תף, drum)
5. *Machol* (מחול, dance)
6. *Minim* (מנים, organ)
7. *Ugav* (עגב, flute)
8. *Tziltzlei shama* (צלצלי שמע, clanging cymbals)
9. *Tziltzlei teruah* (צלצלי תרועה, sounding trumpets)

The last verse in the psalm reads, "Let all (כל, *kol*) souls praise God, halleluy-a." The word *kol* (all) in this verse hints to the word "voice" (קול, *kol*), since the כ of כל (all) and the ק of קול (voice) are interchangeable. Indeed, the voice, beyond a means of expressing praises musically, is the most harmonic and versatile instrument of all. As there are ten kabbalistic spheres, when we view voice as a musical instrument, we see that each sphere has an instrument with which it corresponds.

ram's horn	שופר	כתר
lute	נבל	חכמה
harp	כנור	בינה
drum	תוף	חסד
dance	גבורה	מחול
organ	מינים	תפארת
flute	עוגב	נצח
clanging cymbals	צלצלי שמע	הוד
sounding cymbals	צלצלי תרועה	יסוד
voice	קול	מלכות

In his illuminating commentary to the Torah, the eleventh-century rabbi, Rabbenu Bachaya, explains that the musical instruments are parallel to the celestial bodies in our solar system. For example the *kinor* equals the planet Saturn, and *toph* equals Jupiter. *Machol* equals the planet Mars, the planet that affects the desert on Earth. This explains the verse in Exodus (32:19): "As soon as he (Moses) came near to the camp he saw the calf and the dancing (*machol*)." The Jews used the *machol* when dancing so that the planet Mars might connect with and affect the desert, where they idolized the Golden Calf.

Further, the *minim* corresponds to the sun, and the *ugav* to the planet Venus. It is interesting to note that דברי עגבים means "objects of love," which is what Venus has been said to represent. The *tziltzelei shama* is parallel to Mercury; the *tziltzelei teruah,* to the moon. Finally, the synthesis of all—the symphony—is Earth, which has elements of each one simultaneously.

Just as each instrument has a corresponding planet, so, too, is each related to the שבעת המינים (*shevat haminim,* the seven species with which the land of Israel was blessed).

(כנור) בינה	–	(נבל) חכמה שעורה	– חטה
(מחול) גבורה		(תוף) חסד	
		(מנים) תפארת	גפן
(צ״שמע) הוד	–	(עוגב) נצח רימון	– תאנה
		(צ״תרועה) יסוד	– זית
		(כל נ..) מלכות	– תמר

(According to one opinion, the fig was the fruit of the Tree of Life. This fruit symbolized eternity, נצח, but man sinned and lost this opportunity.)

Another musical instrument is the *chatzotzra* (חצוצרות, trumpets). The word is made up of two words, חצו (*chatzu,* divided, broken) and צרות (*tzarot,* troubles), because the *chatzotzra* has the power to "break troubles." Indeed, many Hebrew words related to music mean "breaking" for the same reason. For example, *zemer* (זמר, tune) is from לזמר (*lezamer*), meaning to prune or break.

Shir (שיר, melody) means "to shear." *Niggun* (נגון, song) represents power and strength, not unlike the English word "gun." We see from these expressions that music is symbolic of great strength and power.

The explanation of the word *shofar* is that שופר comes from the word לשפר (*leshaper*), to improve, to make something pleasant. שופר is also on par with שפר, which means beauty. שופר is also related to the word ספור (*sipur*), from the word ספר (*sefer,* counting), as well as the word ספיר (*sapir,* sapphire), because the ש of שופר and the ס of ספור, are sibilant letters that are interchangeable (i.e., they are produced by expelling air between the teeth). ספיר is also related to the soul, and, according to Kabbalah, is the root of the נשמה (*neshama,* soul, spirit). ספר (*sefer,* book) is also related to the spirit, for the spirit is like a book in which all man's deeds are recorded. Notice the similarity of the English word "spirit" to ספיר, ספירות. The *Ohr Hachaim Hakodesh* says that all souls are engraved on, and are taken from, the heavenly ספיר.

CHAPTER 2

The Shofar

The four sounds of the *shofar* (ram's horn) blown on Rosh Hashana describe the stages that the soul of mankind experiences. The four sounds are תקיעה (*tekiya,* a single long blast), שברים (*shevarim,* three shorter blasts), תרועה (*teruah,* a series of many shorter blasts) and תקיעה גדולה (*tekia gedola,* "the great tekia," one very long blast). The first *tekia* represents the original state of man before the sin, when he was still "straight," as it says in Ecclesiastes (7:29): והא–לקים עשה את האדם ישר והמה בקשו חשבונות רבים; "God created man straight, but they searched for numerous calculations." The souls were still straight and unbroken.

The *shevarim* represents the soul of man immediately after the first sin—i.e., the broken spirit symbolized by broken continuity of three short blasts. Later, man realized the ramifications that the sin and its punishment caused—the fall of man and the tainting of Creation. Thus, man's spirit was shattered into fragments of its original splendor. This is symbolized by the disjointed series of short blasts. However, repentance regained for man the beauty of his original glory. Though regaining and reestablishing man's once-exalted position is a slow and difficult process for an individual and for mankind, it is surely an attainable goal. Indeed, the Jewish nation as a whole reached the level of man before the sin when they heard the *shofar* (ram's horn) and the direct word of God on Mount Sinai.

The long, slow process of straightening out the soul is symbolized by the final sound of the *shofar* blown on Rosh Hashana—the single long blast.

The fact that the *shofar* (ram's horn) has great power can be seen in a number of ways. The word שופר (*shofar*) is actually made up of two terms: ש and פר. The letter ש represents light and glory. The word פר (*par*, bull) denotes power. Thus, the שופר implies a glorious power. The letter פ (Peh) represents the mouth, which is connected to the heart, and the letter ר (Resh) represents the head (ראש), which is connected to the brain. The שפר causes a brightness (i.e., purity) of the brain and the heart.

The power of the שופר (*shofar*, ram's horn) was used as a spiritual and physical weapon at the time of the prophet Joshua when he led the Jews to conquer the city of Jericho. The *shofar*s were blown and the walls of the city crumbled. The walls of the city represent the קליפות (*klipot*, impure shells) that hide the inner divine core the way a nut is hidden by its shell. Jericho was the center of all idolatry and evil forces at the time. Each of the seven idolatrous nations living in the land of Israel at that time had representatives there.

The inner letters of the word יריחו (Yericho, Jericho) are ריח (*re'ach*, spirit). It is necessary to break the impure shell to release the inner spirit. Thus, at Jericho, a paradigm of the victory of good over evil was displayed to the world through the Jewish people. The walls of Jericho, which represent the קליפות (*klipot*), were broken and the spirit was released. The *shofar*'s ability to break through those barriers was used to uplift the spirit. Notice that when we replace the פ of שופר with the letter ב (interchangeable, as both are labial letters), we are left with the word שובר (*shover*, breaks). Hence the *shofar*, the first of the musical instruments, has the ability to destroy evil forces.

The *gematria* of the root of *shofar* is 580 (שפר; 300 + 80 + 200 = 580). The number 580 is also the value of the word תפילין (*tefillin*, phylacteries; 400 + 80 + 10 + 30 + 10 + 50 = 580). The *tefillin* bind our heart and mind to God and are our spiritual ornaments. *Tefillin*, simply stated, are boxes, made of animal skin, that contain the verses in the Torah that deal with God's unity, written on parchment. The verse "Hear, o Israel, Hashem is our God, Hashem is One" (Deuteronomy, 6:4) and the verses that follow are written there. One aspect of this *mitzvah* is to teach that man must use his entire ability to work and create (symbolized by the box shape, a shape not usually found in nature, but the model of a man-made object such as a table, window, or book), to elevate his animal nature (denoted by the leather and animal-based materials of the *tefillin*) by binding (the *tefillin* knots) his heart and mind (the head *tefillin* facing the mind, and the arm *tefillin* facing the heart) to God ("God is One" on the parchment). The *shofar* (ram's horn, which is also taken from an animal) connotes beauty, like the *tefillin,* which are like jewelry. *Shofar* also suggests connecting and uniting with God, as does *tefillin,* which contains the verses about God's unity. The simple *gematria* is taken by ignoring the zeroes of a word. Thus, *shofar* (שפר = 3 + 8 + 2) is equal to 13, which is the *gematria* of אחד (*echad,* one). Also, the small *gematria* of *shofar* and *tefillin,* taken by adding the digits of the full *gematria,* is equal to 13, again the unity (580 = 5 + 8 + 0 = 13). These expressions of God's unity bring one to אהבה (*ahava,* love), which is also 13, again the unity (1 + 5 + 2 + 5 = 13).

The number 580 also has its negative aspect. סמא-ל (Sama'el, the evil angel) poisons the mind with סם (*sam,* poison, drugs). The heart is under attack by the force of לילית (Lilit, the evil temper). The *gematria* of סם and לילית together equal 580 (סם = 60 + 40 = 100; לילית = 30 + 10 + 30 + 10 + 400 = 480; 480 + 100 = 580). The *shofar* (ram's horn) and *tefillin* have the power to fight these forces. They are our spiritual weapons in the celestial war. The head *tefillin* conquer the סם (*sam*), and the *tefillin* of the arm opposite the heart destroys the power of לילית (Lilit).

The *shofar* (ram's horn) is unique among the musical instruments in that, through it, we fulfill a specific *mitzvah,* that of blowing the *shofar* on Rosh Hashana. This is called תקע בשופר (*t'ka b'shofar,* blowing the *shofar*). The word תקע comes from the word עתיק (*atik,* ancient), which alludes to a very high sphere, since God is the most ancient, having preceded all of Creation and being infinite. The numerical value of עתיק is also 580, the same as the *shofar,* so we see a close connection (70 + 400 + 10 + 100 = 580).

CHAPTER 3

The Nevel

The *nevel* (lute) of King David was somewhat similar to a modern harp or lyre. The *nevel* leads one to wisdom. The small *gematria* of *nevel* (נבל; 50 + 2 + 30 = 82 = 8 + 2 = 10) is equal to the small *gematria* of חכמה (*chochma,* wisdom; 8 + 20 + 40 + 5 = 73 = 7 + 3 = 10). This number can be reduced even further, to 1 (10 = 1 + 0 = 1). "One" represents the One and only God. A verse in Proverbs states: ראשית חכמה יראת ה'; "The beginning of wisdom is the fear of God." So, the *nevel* can help one in his quest for divine wisdom.

The word נבל (*nevel,* lute) has the same letters as the word לבן (*lavan,* white). White light contains all of the seven colors of the spectrum. This can be demonstrated by passing a beam of white light through a prism, which splits the light into its component parts. Similarly, חכמה (*chochma,* wisdom) contains, and is the starting point for, other forms of knowledge and understanding. The word חכמה consists of two terms כח (*koach,* power) and מה (*mah,* what)—i.e., the power of asking questions and obtaining knowledge.

There is an interesting connection between *nevel* (lute) and the word נבל (*naval,* vile, mean). Our Sages tell us that the *nevel* is such a beautiful instrument, it puts the other instruments to shame. This idea is further revealed by exchanging the ב in נבל for a פ (ב and פ are interchangeable, as labial letters). Thus, we arrive at the word נפל (*nafal,* fallen). Similarly, the word לבן (*lavan,* white) has its negative aspects as well. For example, biblical leprosy (*tzaraat*) is diagnosed by patches of white on the skin (Exodus, 4:6). Similarly, Jacob's father-in-law, Laban, whose name is spelled the same as לבן, is the epitome of a hypocrite, trying to appear righteous but in reality being unfair, immoral, and idolatrous.

Note that cocaine and heroin, two highly destructive drugs, are white powders. This phenomenon can be seen in many places in nature: Though in the medium of light, white is a combination of every color; in the medium of pigments, white is the lack of all color. In contrast, in light, black is the lack of all colors, but in pigments, black is a mixture of all colors. We see, then, that in all of his creations, God gives us the ability to create or destroy, to do good or evil, so that we may choose good and thereby draw closer and closer to his ultimate goodness.

CHAPTER 4

The Kinor

The ancient *kinor* (harp) was shaped like a heart because of the in-strument's close connection to man's heart and soul. The word כנור (*kinor*) has within it the word נר (*ner*, candle), and the number כו (26). The candle represents man's soul, as the nature of the flame is always to soar upwards. The number 26 stands for the Eternal's name, the tetragramaton—י-ה-ו-ה—since it has the *gematria* of 26 (10 + 5 + 6 + 5 = 26). So the soul of a man, his closest connection to God, is strongly affected by the *kinor*; it can be used to direct the heart above.

The *gematria* of כנור is 276 (20 + 50 + 6 + 200 = 276). The small *gematria* is 15 (2 + 7 + 6 = 15), which is equal to 6 (1 + 5 = 6). Six is also the small *gematria* of God's name י-ה (10 + 5 = 15 = 1 + 5 = 6). The letter י represents חכמה (*chochma*, wisdom), and the letter ה rep-resents בינה (*bina*, understanding). Thus, the *kinor* (harp) brings per-fection to חכמה and בינה.

The connection of the כנור (*kinor*, harp) to the attribute of בינה (understanding) can be seen in two verses in Psalm 49. Verse 4 says: פי ידבר חכמות והגות לבי תבונות; "My mouth will speak wisdom, and the meditation of my heart, understanding." In this case, חכמה precedes בינה. Verse 5 continues: אטה למשל אזני, אפתח בכנור חידתי; "I will incline my ear to a parable, and will solve my problem with a *kinor*." From here, we can see that the כנור has the ability to solve problems, which leads to understanding.

The נבל (*nevel*, lute) and כנור (*kinor*, harp) are often found to-gether, as in Psalms (57:9 and 108:3): נבל וכנור; "a *nevel* and a *kinor*."

The נבל, being parallel to the attribute of חכמה (*chochma,* wisdom), corresponds to the י of Hashem's name, and the כנור to בינה (*bina,* understanding) and to the ה of Hashem's name, forming an intimate couple.

Their connection can be seen further by their combined numerical value (כנור + נבל = 50 + 2 + 30, + 20 + 50 + 6 + 200 = 358), which has the same value as משיח (40 + 300 + 10 + 8 = 358; *Moshiach,* the Messiah). This shows that the time of *Moshiach* will bring a unification of wisdom and understanding that will fill the land, as can be seen from the verse (Isaiah, 11:9): מלאה הארץ דעה את ה' כמים לים מכסים; "The earth will be filled with knowledge just as water covers the sea."

CHAPTER 5

The Combination of Shofar, Nevel, and Kinor

The *shofar* (ram's horn), *nevel* (lute), and *kinor* (harp) share a special relationship. These three musical instruments are parallel to the three attributes of כתר (*keter,* crown), חכמה (*chochma,* wisdom), and בינה (*bina,* understanding). The unity of these three, and the unity one may achieve by using them, is seen by taking the small *gematria* of the combined values. The combined value is 760 (כתר = 620, חכמה = 73, בינה = 67; 620 + 73 + 67 = 760). The small *gematria* of 760 is 13 (7 + 6 + 0 = 13), which is the *gematria* of אחד (*echad,* one).

The relationship between a group of words can be revealed by combining the initials to form a word. The initials of שופר, כנור, and נבל are שכ"נ, which has the same root as שכינה (*Shechina,* the divine Presence). The revelation of the שכינה, as a result of music, can be observed in the inner numerical value of the letters of the word שירה (*shira,* song), which, fully spelled out, are יש, וד,·ין, הה ,ריש, יוד, שין (יש, ה = 10 + 50, + 6 + 4, + 10 + 300, + 5 = 385), the same as that of שכינה (300 + 20 + 10 + 50 + 5 = 385). This indicates that the revelation of the divine Presence is contained within music. The משכן (*Mishkan,* tabernacle), built as a place of worship by the ancient Jews in the Sinai Desert, was so called because God dwelt there.

The *gematria* of שכ"ן is 370 (300 + 20 + 50 = 370). This is the same as the *gematria* of the word שלם (*shalem,* perfect: 300 + 30 + 40 = 370). The number 370 is also the numerical value of the letters שע, which mystically refer to the 370 lights (*Kehilat Yaakov,* שע). ישועה (*yeshua,* salvation) is made up of the three letters of Hashem's name—ה-ו-י—and the שע. Thus, salvation is a result of the full divine enlightenment. So, a man has not reached perfection until he has mastered the qualities of the שופר (shofar, ram's horn), כנור (kinor, harp) and נבל (nevel, lute), which are כתר (keter), בינה (bina), and חכמה (chochma).

The number 370 also represents perfection of the ten spheres. There are three upper spheres—כתר, חכמה, and בינה—and seven lower ones, which allude to the seven celestial bodies that affect nature. The number 370 contains three units of 100, which represent the three upper spheres. The 70, seven units of ten, corresponds to the lower spheres and to the seventy nations, seventy elders of the *Sanhedrin,* etc. The word חכמה (8 + 20 + 40 + 5) has a numerical value of 73. Again, the digits 7 and 3 remind us that חכמה is a necessary quality for anyone embarking on a journey into the realm of spiritual knowledge.

In traditional Jewish mysticism, one may learn valuable lessons by analyzing the last letters of the words in a sentence or phrase. For example, if we take the last letters of the words in the Torah that begin the account of the Creation of the world (Genesis, 1:1): בראשית ברא א-לקים; "In the beginning, God created," we obtain the letters ת, א, and מ, which spell the word אמת (*emet,* truth), to show that the world was created based on truth.

The last three words of the account of the creation (Genesis, 2:3) are: ברא א-לקים לעשות (God blessed the seventh day and declared it holy, for in it he rested from all the work from which) "God had created and performed." These words also end with the letters אמת. Notice that the word אמת consists of the first letter of the alphabet, א, the middle letter, מ, and the last letter, ת. This teaches that truth is all-inclusive, fixed and immovable, and true. The fact that the last letters of the last phrase of the account of Creation spell the word אמת teach us that truth will always triumph, prevail, and conquer in the end. This is made obvious by the history of Israel. Mighty nations, civilizations, cities, and cultures rise and fall, but the modest Jew, with his holy Torah, remains standing. The vast empires of the Greeks, Egyptians, Persians, and Romans, not to mention innumerable smaller kingdoms, have crumbled to dust. Their evil decrees and persecutions of our people have failed on the merit of our steadfast dedication to Torah. Even after countless innocents have been murdered, tortured, raped, robbed, and massacred, our people remain strong. Only to the extent that we have strayed from the Creator's word have the enemies of God and the Jews succeeded. Anyone with patience and foresight could have foreseen the outcome.

In music, the same technique can be used to reveal various teachings. The last letters of the words שופר, נבל, and כינור have a numerical value of 430 (ל, ר, ר = 200 + 200 + 30 = 430). This is a highly significant number, as we shall see. The small *gematria* is equal to 7 (4 + 3 + 0 = 7), which is the number of notes in the musical scale. The number 430 is also the value of the word נפש (*nefesh,* the first part of the soul; 50 + 80 + 300 = 430). So, making music with the combination of the שופר, נבל, and כינור can help bring out the נפש and lead one to a נפש שלם, a complete spirit. The number 430, the inner numerical value of the letters of the word פאר (*p'er,* harmony and beauty; פי, אלף, ריש–י, לף, יש = 10, + 30 + 80, + 10 + 300 = 430), is the same as נפש, teaching us that the purity and beauty of the נפש is revealed through harmony.

We have seen that the soul contains five parts, the נפש (*nefesh*), רוח (*ruach*), and נשמה (*neshama*), and the יחידה (*yechida*) and חי–ה (*chaya*). If we take the number five and multiply it by the value of God's name א-לקים, 86 (1 + 30 + 5 + 10 + 40 = 86), we return to the number 430 (5 × 86 = 430). The number 430 is also the amount of years the Jewish people were to have been slaves in Egypt (Genesis, 15:13): "And (God) said to Abraham, 'Know surely that thy seed shall be strangers in a land that is not theirs and shall be enslaved and inflicted four hundred years, and also that nation whom they shall serve I shall judge, and afterwards they shall come out with a great wealth.'" After the years of servitude to Egypt, the Jews received the Torah, and their servitude was redirected to God. Thus, the נפש underwent a process of perfection.

CHAPTER 6

The Toph

The next instrument mentioned in Psalm 150 is the תוף (*toph*), which represents חסד (*chesed*). התף (*hatoph,* the drum), has the same letters as פתה (*pata,* tempted). If we replace the ה with a ח (interchangeable, as guttural letters), we are left with the word פתוח (*patuach,* open). פתוח is the positive side, the connection of the *toph* to *chesed. Chesed* is represented by open hands and open doors. פתה is the negative side, the temptation and the evil inclination. The numerical value of תף is 490 (400 + 90). The value of חם (*chom,* heat) is 48 (8 + 40). So, 480 is ten times heat, which refers to strong temptation.

Exodus (15:20) says: "Miriam the prophetess, Aaron's sister, took the *toph* in her hand and all the women followed her with *toph*s and *machol*s." The expression "took the *toph* in her hand" implies control over and mastery over evil forces. After they witnessed the splitting of the Red Sea, when great miracles occurred, the people were in control of their desires.

The number 480 is also the value of תלמוד (*talmud,* learning), the Oral Torah (400 + 30 + 40 + 6 + 4 = 480). The Talmud states that God "created an evil inclination within man but also created Torah study as its cure." Thus, by directing one's energy into the most positive direction, the most positive results will follow.

The value of the word מח (*moach,* brain) is 48, so that 480 is ten times brain, which represents the perfection of the mind. The Rambam has stated that lust and desire rest most easily in a place void of wisdom. The force of lust seeks to dwell in the place of least resistance. Thus, one may control his heart by filling it with deep understanding. It is a central principle of Judaism that man can and should become the master of his heart, and not let his heart be the master of himself.

CHAPTER 7

The Machol

The *machol* was an instrument especially associated with dance. The Targum Onkelos (Aramaic) and the Septuagent (Greek) translate the word as meaning "dance." The *Mechilta* and *Pirkey Rabbi Eliezer* say that it was a musical instrument. Other sources portray it as a hand drum, a tambourine-like cymbal, or clapping.

The *machol* is parallel to the planet Mars and to the sphere of גבורה (*gevurah*, strength). The planet Mars represents war. The word מלחמה (*milchama,* war) contains the letters of the word *machol.* War has a positive connotation, in that we are all engaged in a fight for life against the evil inclination. The planet Mars, מאדים, in Hebrew has the root letters of אדום (*adom,* red). This is because Mars, the red planet, represents war.

When a man falls into the habit of doing a certain sin, it is a battle royal to break the habit. Our Sages showed deep insight into human nature when they stated that the first time a man does a particular sin, he feels regret; if he does it again, he feels less regret; and by the third time, he feels that he is already doing a *mitzvah.* To pull oneself out of such a rut is a real battle, and can be viewed as a life-or-death struggle, for his portion in the world-to-come is at stake. Ben Zoma alluded to this battle when he said, "Which person is truly strong? The one who overcomes the evil inclination" (*Ethics of the Fathers,* 4:1). The struggle to atone is hinted at in the letters of the word *machol,* which also has the same letters as the word מחילה (*mechila,* forgiveness). When man at last repents and turns toward the path of righteousness, no matter how base were his previous actions, he will be forgiven. (It should be pointed out that certain sins require an additional rectification—for example, a thief must also pay back his victims.) Just as one who is ישר (*yashar,* straight) can sing (ישיר, *yashir*), so one who gains forgiveness (מחילה) can dance (מחול).

The word *machol* has the same root letters and the same *gematria* as the word לחם (*lechem,* bread; 30 + 8 + 40 = 78). Let us examine the significance of the number 78. Seventy-eight has a small *gematria* of 15 (7 + 8), which is the value of God's name י–ה (10 + 5). In Jewish law, on the Sabbath, one makes the blessing over bread for a meal on משנה לחם (*lechem mishnah,* two loaves of bread). This is reminiscent of the double portion of manna that fell from heaven on Fridays so that the Jews would not gather manna on the Sabbath. Thus, if we multiply the value of לחם by two, we get 156 (2 × 78). The number 156 is also the value of אהל מועד (*ohel moed,* the communion tent of the tabernacle; 1 + 5 + 30 + 90 + 6 + 70 + 4 = 156). The number 156 is also the value of ציון (Zion), the place where the Temple permanently remains.

The word מלח (*melach,* salt) also has a value of 78. In Jewish custom, one dips bread into salt three times before eating. Salt was used in the Temple service, and we use it together with bread on our dining tables to signify sanctity. Three times the value of the tetragrammaton is 78 (26 × 3), which is the value of both לחם (*lechem,* bread) and מלח (*melach,* salt). The combined value of לחם and מלח is, again, 156. So we see that many musical terms in general, and *machol* in particular, have numerical values that are congruent with Divinity and with supernal ideas.

CHAPTER 8

The Minim

Rabbi Shimshon Raphael Hirsch says that the *minim* is an instrument used to express the more quiet rejoicing of the individual. The *minim* is parallel to the sphere of תפארת (*tiferet,* beauty), which is the centrally located sphere. תפארת is the central sphere and represents harmony; harmony of forces, harmony of patterns, and harmony of music. The word מינים (*minim*) is a synonym, and also means different kinds—plural of the word מין (*min,* kind).

CHAPTER 9

The Ugav

The *ugav* is parallel to the planet Venus, and to the sphere of נצח (*netzach*, eternity). The numerical value of עוגב is 81 (70 + 6 + 3 + 2). Eighty-one is also the value of כסא (*kisai*, chair; 20 + 60 + 1), which represents the כסא הכבוד (*Kisai HaKavod*, the Throne of Glory; see Ezekiel, 1:26; Isaiah, 6:1). The word כסא is actually made up of two terms: כס (*kas*, a covering) and א, which represents God. This refers to nature (טבע, *teva*), which also has a *gematria* of 81 (9 + 2 + 70). Nature and the natural world are the garments of God. God does not reveal himself to us directly; such a revelation would be unbearable for flesh and blood. Instead, the physical world is given to many to relate to God indirectly. When God acts to reward or punish, he does it through nature. The spiritual person will understand the higher source from whence the nature comes, and the irreligious will attribute it to nature alone. For example, God may choose to punish the evil by sending a new disease to earth, one that affects only drug addicts, prostitutes, and the like. Yet the Godless will still look into their microscopes and say, "This virus causes the epidemic," and ignore the first cause. Has not King Solomon warned us (Proverbs, 26:13), "A prudent man sees the evil and hides himself, but the simpletons continue and are punished," and (Ecclesiastes, 7:13), "Consider the work of God, for who can make straight that which he has made crooked."

Thus, the *ugav* is closely related to one's material tendencies, which, if left out of control, can be destructive.

On a positive side, *ugav* also has the same value as אנכי (*anochi*, I am), which is the first word of the Ten Commandments (Exodus, 20:2): אנכי ה' א–לקיך; "I am Hashem your God."

אנכי also refers to one's inner self. Thus, the *ugav* can bring out one's spiritual self, his supersensory potential.

The number 81 has the same digits as 18, which shows a close relationship. Eighteen is the value of חי (*chai*, life). The letter ח, which stands for חי, also stands for חטא (*chet*, sin), which is the negative aspect of this letter. Notice that the English words live, evil, veil, and vile all have the same letters. One can say that if one does not live properly, but covers his own goodness with a veil (קליפות, *klipot*, shells), he becomes evil and, thus, becomes vile. In English, such wordplay is a game, but in Hebrew, לשון הקודש (*lashon hakodesh*, the holy tongue), one can examine every word and discover deep relationships between seemingly unrelated concepts. One can learn many mystical and moral lessons by gathering the sparks of the holy tongue.

CHAPTER 10

The Tziltzelei Shama and the Tziltzelei Teruah

The *tziltzelei shama* is parallel to the planet Mercury. The word *shama* relates to the left side of our map of attributes. The attribute of בינה (*bina*) is on the left, and *shama* connotes understanding, as in the verse (Deuteronomy, 6:4): שמע ישרא-ל, ה' א-לקנו ה' אחד; "Hear (understand), o Israel, Hashem is our God, Hashem is One." According to Kabbalah (ספר היצירה, *Sefer Hayetzirah,* the book of Creation, which is said to have been written by our forefather, Abraham), each planet was created with a specific letter of the alphabet, the letter that connotes its influence and character. The planet Mercury's letter is ר, which is the first letter of the word רץ (*ratz,* run). In English, many words that imply fast movement begin with this sound as well (run, rush, race, rapid). So the *tziltzelei shama* is related to quick temper, fast movement. Indeed, the planet Mercury has the smallest orbit of any other planet in our solar system, and has the fastest year. (A year is how long it takes a planet to revolve around the sun one time.) A year in Mercury is 88 days long, as opposed to Earth, whose year is 365½ days long. Interestingly, a day on Mercury takes forty Earth-days to complete, so while a Mercury year is 88 Earth-days long, a Mercury year is only 2.2 Mercury-days long. (A day is how long it takes a planet to revolve on its axis one time.)

The *tziltzelei teruah* is related to the sphere of יסוד (*yesod,* foundation). The word תרועה (*terua*) has the same root letters as רעות (*reut,* friendship), as the Torah relates (Leviticus, 19:18): ואהבתך לרעך כמוך; "Love your neighbor as yourself." The *tziltzelei teruah* cultivates friendship and peace. Peace is the apex of the priestly blessing mentioned in the Torah (Numbers, 6:24): "May God bless you and keep you; may God make his face shine upon you and be gracious to you; may God lift up his countenance to you and give you peace." So, during the service of the Temple in Jerusalem, we see that while the Levites were singing praises to God and playing musical instruments, which cultivated harmony and friendship, the Kohanim were simultaneously blessing the people with peace.

Conclusion

Judaism and the Hebrew language, the holy tongue, are vast and deep, embracing incomprehensible knowledge of every aspect and sphere of life. One can only scratch the surface, as it were, to realize the depth and beauty of the divine language and way of life. Even though this book deals with numerous subjects and ideas, it is by no means all-encompassing, but is simply meant as a glimpse of its profound beauty and depth.

Index

Levi Yitzchak of Berdichev, 59
Luria, Isaac, 35
Lute (*nevel*)
  combinations, 91–93
  described, 87–88

Machol, described, 97–98
Melody, terminology, 55–59
Minim, described, 99
Mozart, W. A., 58
Musical instruments. *See*
  Instruments
Musical scale, 3–28
  first scale elaboration,
    21–24
  four scale rationale, 19–20
  Hebrew vowels, 9–12
  octave relationships, 13–15
  second scale elaboration,
    25–26
  seven-letter cycle, 3–8
  supernatural and, 17–18
  third scale elaboration,
    27–28
Musical terminology. *See*
  Terminology

Nachman of Breslav, 58
Nevel (lute)
  combinations, 91–93
  described, 87–88

Octave relationships, musical
  scale, 13–15

Poetic song, terminology, 47
Power, harmony and beauty,
  terminology, 43–45

Praise, for natural and
  miraculous, terminology,
  61–64

Scale. *See* Musical scale
Schubert, F., 58
Second scale elaboration,
  musical scale, 25–26
Seven-letter cycle, musical scale,
  3–8
Shabbat songs, 107
Shneur Zalman of Liadi, 58
Shofar
  combinations, 91–93
  described, 83–85
Simple tune, terminology, 35–41
Song
  eternity and, terminology,
    65–66
  meaning of, terminology,
    49–54
  poetic, terminology, 47
Spirituality, praise, 61–64
Supernatural scale, 17–18

Terminology, 31–75
  harmony, beauty, and power,
    43–45
  joy, expressions of, 71–75
  melody, 55–59
  overview of, 31–33
  praise, 61–64
  simple tune, 35–41
  song
    eternity and, 65–66
    meaning of, 49–54
    poetic, 47
  voice, uniqueness of, 67–69

Third scale elaboration, musical
   scale, 27–28
Toph, described, 95–96
Tziltzelei shama and *tziltzelei
   teruah,* described, 103–104

Ugav, described, 101–102

Voice, uniqueness of,
   terminology, 67–69

About the Author

Rabbi Matityahu Glazerson was born and educated in Israel. He studied at Medrashiat Noam in Pardes Chana, and at various yeshivot, including Kfar Chassidim, Ponievez, and Chevron. Today he is involved in teaching in a Kollel, and lecturing at various institutions, like Neve Yerushalayim, Ma'ayonot Yerushalayim, and Kol B'Rama. He is instrumental in paving a new way toward the instillment of Jewish values. Rabbi Glazerson is the author of many books including *The Secrets of the Haggadah; Torah, Light, and Healing: Mystical Insights into Healing Based on the Hebrew Language; Above the Zodiac: Astrology in Jewish Thought;* and *Building Blocks of the Soul: Studies on the Letters and Words of the Hebrew Language.*